D0175366

THE ART OF THE ADVANTAGE

THE ART
OF THE
ADVANTAGE

優勝之道

36 STRATEGIES TO SEIZE
THE COMPETITIVE EDGE

Kaihan Krippendorff

THOMSON
— ✴ —™
TEXERE

Australia · Canada · Mexico · Singapore · Spain · United Kingdom · United States

The Art of the Advantage: 36 Strategies to Seize the Competitive Edge
Kaihan Krippendorff

COPYRIGHT © 2003 by Kaihan Krippendorff
Published in the U.K. by the Penguin Group

Published in 2003 by TEXERE, part of the Thomson Corporation. TEXERE, Thomson, and Thomson logo are trademarks used herein under license.

ISBN 1-58799-168-3

Printed in the United States of America
1 2 3 4 5 6 7 08 09 07 06 05 04 03

For more information, contact Texere, 300 Park Avenue South, New York, NY 10010 or find us on the Web at www.etexere.com.

Contents

PART ONE

YIN YANG: POLARITY

陰陽

PART TWO

WU WEI: GO WITH THE GRAIN

無為

PART THREE

WU CHANG: CONTINUOUS CHANGE

無常

PART FOUR

SHANG BING WU BING: INDIRECT ACTION

上兵無兵

Acknowledgments

Out of interest and curiosity, I had been compiling business cases for several years when, in 1998, my strategy professor at Columbia Business School, Kathryn Harrigan, planted the idea that I might be writing a book. I thank her for setting me on the path. Along the way countless business minds contributed to my exploration. Professors Bob Bontempo (Columbia Business School), Ming-Jer Chen (Darden School of Business), Costas Markides (London Business School), Sumantra Ghoshal (London Business School), and Keith Weigelt (Wharton Business School) listened to and shaped my ideas. Mark McNeilly and Richard D'Aveni sharpened my focus. Juan-Jose Gonzalez, Brad Hoover, Tim Lukes, and Joanna Popper propelled me forward with their passion.

To truly understand the subtleties of the 36 stratagems, however, requires that one have a Chinese heritage, a degree in Chinese studies, or patient friends. I luckily had the third. Qin Chen spent days with me explaining and critiquing my interpretation of each stratagem. Christina Zhu energetically answered my innumerable questions and reviewed my manuscript. Teresa Chu, Harry Wang, Steve Heine, and Alex Tsui kept my interpretation of the Chinese philosophy behind each stratagem on target. Bill Barnet, Dietrich Chen, Gerry Garcia, Arun Iyer, Nissim Jabiles, Jeff Kvaal, David Wenner, and many of those named here generously reviewed my final manuscript. Their time made a bigger difference than they think.

I thank Victoria Larson, my editor at Texere, for her dedication to this book, for her patience in working with a first-time author and for her guidance in the book's editorial structure. I also thank Mark Ledden and Katie Ruben for their editorial contributions.

Three people took particularly firm stands that this book would be written: Laurie Harper, my agent, believed in my idea and fought persistently for its realization. Without her in my corner this book would not be. Jacques Antebi shared my ideas and pushed me forward at every opportunity. Gervase Warner showed only passionate conviction.

I thank my mother and father, Sultana Alam and Klaus Krippendorff, who always believed in and encouraged my dreams. Their constant and genuine interest in the book and our hours of engaging conversation enriched its content, expanded its scope and enlivened the process. My stepmother, Marge Thorell, who, in the early stages, invested many hours smoothing and tightening my prose. My sister, Heike Sullivan, my cousins, aunts, and uncles in Philadelphia who never doubted that I would finish this book. Last but always first, I cannot adequately thank my wife and soul mate, Pilar Ramos, who stood by me throughout, even on sunny Sundays, untangling my thoughts and toying with new ideas.

KAIHAN KRIPPENDORFF
MIAMI, FLORIDA
NOVEMBER, 2002

Preface

WHEN I FIRST HAPPENED UPON a translation of *The 36 Stratagems*, I asked myself whether this ancient Chinese text could play a role in today's business world. After analyzing almost three hundred contemporary business case studies through the lens of *The 36 Stratagems*, I concluded that these stratagems are both relevant to today and are powerful tools for competing and winning the complex game of business.

The 36 Stratagems is a text that offers us new perspectives about how to influence, gain, and maintain an advantage over our competitors. It does not advocate force necessarily but rather it expands our imagination thereby allowing us to generate consistently creative options and strategies so helpful in our increasingly competitive and tightly-woven world. Creative strategies are more important than ever in today's information-driven society with its increasingly fluid boundaries of competition brought about by, among other factors, lower communication costs and accelerated technology developments. Product life cycles are shorter, cross-industry rivalry is growing, and the increasing number of competitors is forcing players to specialize. The result is a faster-paced, more dynamic game with similar characteristics to the conflicts that birthed *The 36 Stratagems* during China's Warring States period (475–221 B.C.). This book will show that the 36 stratagems are as effective in contemporary business as they have proven to be in ancient Chinese warfare. Companies including Microsoft, Sony, and Coca-Cola already use them, albeit unknowingly, to win their most contentious battles.

Two interests drew me initially to *The 36 Stratagems*. The first was a curiosity about Eastern philosophy that began when I was ten years old, and I started studying Chinese martial arts. A few years later, my father, who is a communications professor, introduced me to Taoism and Zen Buddhism. Since then I have continued to explore the philosophies of East and South Asia, encouraged by my mother and her family, who are from South Asia.

The second reason for my interest in *The 36 Stratagems* was their potential to create powerful business strategies. While at Wharton, Columbia, and London business schools, I found the most interesting stories to be those of companies that beat their competition with innovative approaches, many times with fewer resources. Sure, size can be a guarantee for long-term profits and an important factor in securing a sustainable competitive advantage as De Beers demonstrated with diamonds, or Alcoa did with steel. But such opportunities are less common in today's information age. The alternative form of competition: Outmaneuvering the competition by sustaining a sequence of temporary advantages can ensure companies consistent success.

I was excited when I realized that *The 36 Stratagems* contains the playbook for winning the fast-paced game of business. I was further encouraged by the fact that *The 36 Stratagems* are still relatively unknown outside of China. The West has embraced Sun Tzu's *The Art of War*, but we are still unfamiliar with its sister text, *The 36 Stratagems*. Crafted and proven in the past, *The 36 Stratagems* speaks to humankind's unchanging nature. Despite the Industrial Revolution, the Information Age and the Internet's potential, the new games we think we are discovering actually have ancient and long-forgotten precedents. We thought we were entering a "new economy" based on new rules but have discovered, often painfully, that the rules of the game have not changed. Business, like politics and life itself, is based on the same permanent principles of power and survival. Human nature has not changed, and the proven tactics of the past remain relevant today.

Universal Maneuvers

M ORE THAN 2,500 YEARS AGO, military and political minds in China began to debate how to make a science of strategy by distilling their collective knowledge into a few universal principles. The process took more than a thousand years, and it produced a highly-synthesized catalog of thirty-six tactics for gaining, expanding, and retaining power: *The 36 Stratagems*. Less famous in the West than many of its sister texts, including Sun Tzu's *The Art of War*, Lao Tzu's *Tao Te Ching*, and the most ancient of Chinese classical texts, the *I Ching*, *The 36 Stratagems* is no less an important and permanent part of Chinese strategic thought. Even today, the Chinese commonly refer to *The 36 Stratagems* within the contexts of family, office, national, and international politics. The stratagems are not taught formally; rather they live in Chinese oral tradition as they have for centuries. Many argue that Chinese and Japanese businesses executives consciously use *The 36 Stratagems* to craft corporate strategy.

The 36 Stratagems compiles the lessons of more than twenty generations. By comparison, most strategic texts capture the lessons of little more than a lifetime. This book compresses this information, even more completely than other texts, into only one hundred and thirty-eight Chinese characters. Each short phrase packs in volumes of learning that its user can unwrap through creative interpretation.

To appreciate the amount of experience recorded in *The 36 Stratagems*, consider what the known world's cultures experienced over the course of the stratagems' formation:

- Athens rose to dominate Greece and was then defeated by Macedonia's Alexander the Great

- The Roman Empire was founded and expanded into Greece, Persia, the Middle East, and North Africa, eventually conquering the Greek Empire

- The Persian Empire rose to power, and, 500 years later, fell to Rome

- Prince Siddartha Gautama was born in India, took the name Buddha, and founded Buddhism

- Christianity was born and 400 years later, Islam followed

- China generated some its greatest thinkers including Lao Tzu, Sun Tzu, and Confucius and experienced the transition of eleven dynasties. It built the Great Wall and the Silk Road

The true age of *The 36 Stratagems* is difficult to pinpoint because it has no single author. Rather hundreds of politicians, military leaders, and citizens contributed to its development by passing stories down through generations, distilling and refining them with each telling until their bare essences remained. The storytelling that gives us *The 36 Stratagems* began sometime before 500 B.C. and was completed sometime between A.D. 500, when the text was first mentioned in historical records, and about A.D. 1600, when an unknown "author" compiled the stratagems into a handwritten book titled *The Secret Art of War: The 36 Stratagems.*

The text of *The 36 Stratagems* belongs to the same body of military works as Sun Tzu's *The Art of War* and is closely linked to Taoist texts, such as Lao Tzu's *Tao Te Ching*, and to the oldest Chinese classic, the *I Ching. The 36 Stratagems*, *The Art of War*, and *Tao Te Ching*, all of which teach readers how to navigate and gain advantage in dynamic environments, were products of a turbulent period in China's history known as the Warring States period. This period began when a loosely-unified China splintered into separate states that battled each other for power. Seven states quickly dominated the others, and for the next two hundred years they engaged in a dynamic sequence of battles, shifting alliances, and political gaming. Leaders and scholars of this period naturally pondered how to succeed in complex, dynamic environments, and the result was *The Art of War,* the *Tao Te Ching,* and *The 36 Stratagems.*

The Art of War by Sun Tzu is a famous treatise on military strategy. It differs from *The 36 Stratagems* in that it was created by one man, whereas *The 36 Stratagems* were created by many. Sun Tzu provides us with a philosophy and a set of rules, whereas *The 36 Stratagems* addresses implementation, conduct, and actions. It is most likely, however, that Sun Tzu was aware of *The 36 Stratagems,* and that it probably influenced his thinking and vice versa. Westerners may be surprised to see the *Tao Te Ching* grouped with military works because we tend to view the text as promoting a philosophy of noninterference. Many people who consider the *Tao Te Ching* a military tome note its tactical bent and that twenty of its eighty-one chapters directly or indirectly address military issues. Most scholars, however, interpret the text as advocating a philosophy of skilled influence. It teaches us to respect nature's power, and to work with it rather than against it. Above all, the *Tao Te Ching* leads us to influence the universe intelligently, efficiently, and effectively. *The 36 Stratagems* does capture many of the *Tao Te Ching*'s Taoist principles and Sun Tzu's military principles, but the book differs in that it offers options rather than principles, and it distills more information more concisely.

A modern business strategy book, or military text, typically advocates one approach, e.g., the customer is always right, or always attack your competitor's weakest point. *The 36 Stratagems,* however, offers multiple, often contradictory choices, such as, "Surround your enemy," and then "retreat." It *gives* you choices but does not *make* them for you. One might say that while most strategy books restrict options to simplify the game, *The 36 Stratagems* is the complete play book. *The 36 Stratagems* is designed to help us outmaneuver our opponents, to help us craft creative strategies and become superior strategic thinkers.

Some Western leaders may be familiar with Chinese thinking and leadership skills and have incorporated some of these strategies as their own. Many Western corporations also have used the principles of *The 36 Stratagems* albeit not knowingly.

The 36 Stratagems gives us a set of tools to methodically cause us to broaden our thinking and become more creative strategists. Consider that the greatest strategists of our time, whether Western or Eastern, each distinguished himself through creativity. Mao Tse-Tung's methods were so different from his much more powerful adversary they could not adapt to them. Erwin Rommel's uncanny ability to consistently take his adversaries off guard, to keep them guessing incorrectly as to his next move, earned the title the "desert fox." General Nathan Bedford Forrest's moves also seemed impossible to predict. During the U.S. Civil War, he defeated armies multiple times the size of his forces by moving quickly and choosing strategies his northern opponents least expected. The common thread between these and other great military strategists, including Napoleon Bonaparte, is that they saw and chose options their adversaries did not. They thought outside of the boxes that constrain most of us.

The thrust of this book is to summarize the major differences between the Chinese and Western perspectives. *The 36 Stratagems* challenges Westerners to accept a new way of thinking in fundamental ways: Chinese thought pattern assumes an indirect approach, while the West takes the direct approach. The Chinese believe in the holistic relationship between humans and the universe, and that the interdependence of all things is key to our understanding and actions; the West does not. The Chinese conceptualize the world and their environment as cyclical where human interaction and events repeat themselves, whereas the West thinks in terms of isolated "plays," linear causality, and direct influence. For the Chinese, universal principles exist that are applicable in all dimensions, whether they be in nature, politics, war, or personal relations, and there is a constant interaction of the right and left brains. Westerners might recognize the role of coincidence but not a universality of principles or the simultaneous use of right and left brain.

The 36 Stratagems breaks with many Western hidden "laws" of our cultural conditioning that often restrict our thinking and influence our decisions. The stories we heard as children, the books we read, our successes, and our failures influence how we perceive and act as adults. If conditioning is applied objectively, it can help us avoid bad decisions. Ask any venture capitalist if she would rather invest in an entrepreneur who has experienced failure or one who has not. The problem, however, is that we rarely apply our experience objectively or consciously. Rather, we convert our experiences into a bundle of knee-jerk responses (fire = pain, so retract; height = danger, so avoid). These "laws" of response, woven together with thousands of other rules, create our conditioning. They protect us from obvious threats, but often we use them when we should not, and therefore, we make wrong decisions. One way to break our conditioning is to challenge the fundamental "laws" on which it is built. *The 36 Stratagems* offers a simple and effective method for doing this because the stratagems are grounded in Taoist "laws" that are axiomatically different from Western ones.

First Law: Yin Yang/Polarity Westerners believe they can pursue good and banish bad, but this assumption runs counter to the Taoist understanding which doesn't judge "good" and "bad"—they are simply two sides of the same coin.

Second Law: Wu Wei/Go with the Grain Westerners equate yielding with weakness and overcoming adversity with strength. Taoists view the contrary: They value "going with the grain," which often leads us to the opposite answer to the same question.

Third Law: Wu Chang/Continuous Change Westerners believe the past determines the present and that change connects static moments. If Westerners assumed instead that the present determines the present, and that change is continuous, as the Taoist perspective suggests, Westerners would choose different courses of action.

Fourth Law: Shang Bing Wu Bing/Indirect Action Westerners prefer to meet an adversary head-on; the Eastern preference for indirect action often seems impractical, deceitful, or indicative of weakness. Embracing indirect action puts new tactics into Western hands.

IDENTIFYING PATTERNS *The 36 Stratagems* are powerful tools for influencing the outcome of the complex game of "business." Consider business a multiplayer game in which your company interacts with competitors, customers, suppliers, distributors, regulators, and innumerable others. Your goal is to maneuver this web of interdependencies and to cause the outcomes you desire for long-term, substantial profits. *The 36 Stratagems* highlights many of the theories that now are changing the way scientists and economists are attempting to understand the universe. Our traditional approach to explaining nature, using mathematical formulas, is inappropriate and breaks down in trying to explain most systems. For example, many scientists now are exploring "complexity theory" that gives us simple rules and patterns for explaining much of our universe.

Approximately 2,500 years ago, when Lao Tzu introduced Taoism, he advised we study the patterns of nature (e.g., the markings on shells, the patterns of running water, the shapes of trees and clouds) in order to understand and better influence our environments. In the 1970s, scientists from many disciplines—physics, biology, chemistry, mathematics—started identifying patterns in the disorder that they used to classify as "chaos." The result, complexity theory, offers a proposition surprisingly similar to Lao Tzu's: that if we identify a system's patterns, it will make sense; if we understand the patterns, we can then influence the system.

Identifying the patterns of strategic interaction requires looking for patterns in large sets of interactions, such as military battles, political gaming, and business competition, testing the validity of these patterns, synthesizing them, testing the validity of these synthesized patterns, and repeating the process until we have arrived at a limited set of patterns that explain every set of strategic interactions we observe. Identifying an acceptably robust set of patterns for strategic interaction, however, would require studying many centuries of conflict—much more information than our fifty-odd-years' business strategy history provides.

The 36 Stratagems is the best set of patterns we could hope for. It is based on more than one thousand years of information and experience—more than we could ever reasonably expect to build on our own. We will find that the patterns documented in these stratagems actually exist on the battlefield, in the political arena, on the sports field, and in any system in which agents compete for advantage. Learning them enables us to understand and better influence the complex, multiplayer game we call business.

To prove the relevance of *The 36 Stratagems* to business, I tested them against more than 250 contemporary case studies. Appendix B provides a list of these cases as well as the stratagems to which the cases apply. From these cases I selected sixty for inclusion in the book based on these four criteria:

Familiarity I wanted to unveil familiar case studies so that people could view them in alternative ways. To this end I chose well-known cases covered by the media and those most often used to teach strategy in business schools. Ten companies including Asahi, Coca-Cola, Disney, Intel, Krupp, Sony, Nintendo, Flick Brothers/Feldmühle Nobel and Wal-Mart are used by four leading business schools (Wharton, Harvard, London Business School, and Columbia) to teach strategy.

International Application My preference was for global companies that operate in many countries, continents, cultures, and environments.

Entertaining Cases I chose cases that told particularly interesting stories that demonstrate a particular creativity, complexity, and impact.

Illustrative Value I selected cases that most clearly isolated and explained the elements of the stratagem they are meant to illustrate. Many contemporary companies' strategies invoke combinations of the ancient stratagems and so complicate our understanding of the stratagems. To avoid this, the cases presented here are for the most part "pure." Among the cases presented in this book:

COMPANY NAME	# OF CASES	COMPANY NAME	# OF CASES
Alcoa	1	Hindustan-Lever	1
American Beauty	1	Home Depot	1
Asahi	1	Toyota and Honda	1
British Airways	1	Intel	4
Ben and Jerry's	1	Kiwi Airlines	2
Boeing	1	Krupp AG	1
Coke	10	Legend Computer	1
DHL	1	Microsoft	8
Disney	1	Minnetonka	1
Dreamworks SKG	1	Nintendo	2
Epson	1	Sony	5
Flick Brothers/Feldmühle Nobel	1	Southwest Airlines	1
Ford and Chrysler	1	Thomson Travel	1
GE	3	Virgin	5
Gucci	1	Wal-Mart	2

TOTAL NUMBER OF CASES: 60*

* *Some cases involve more than one company*

APPLYING THE STRATAGEMS The stratagems' true meanings can be difficult to grasp. Their differences from one another are often subtle. For example, where a Westerner sees one tactic, Easterners might distinguish three or four permutations. Further complicating our efforts, even Chinese who are familiar with the stratagems can disagree about their "true" meanings. To help you build an understanding of the stratagems, the body of the book presents each stratagem using the original text of *The 36 Stratagems* (but not in the original order), historical stories, modern business cases, and a visual depiction of each stratagem. You may read the body of the work from front to back or pick stratagems at random. Appendix A offers a series of brainstorming questions, or thought-provoking tools, with which you can systematically generate out-of-the-box solutions to your strategic problems.

When first introduced to the stratagems, people often question the ethics of using them. The stratagems are aggressive and often suggest tactics that, at first glance, fall outside of our comfort bounds. There are three reasons, however, to come to terms with, and override this reaction. First, the stratagems are time-tested and proven to be effective in war, politics, and business. Second, if we judge a stratagem before we understand what strategies it might imply, we may rule out an acceptable, winning solution, which would unnecessarily limit our options and weaken our position. Third, these stratagems are in use today by some of the most powerful companies, and they may be used against you. Understanding them will help protect you from being a victim of them. Ultimately, each stratagem can lead us to ethical and unethical courses of action. We should take responsibility for the strategy we choose, not for the stratagem from which it comes. Doing otherwise would unnecessarily diminish our options. This book will help you generate winning options and teach you the art of gaining the advantage.

THE ART OF THE ADVANTAGE

PART ONE

YIN YANG: POLARITY

陰陽

Heaven is yin and yang, cold and hot, the order of the seasons.
Going with it, going against it—this is military victory.[i]

—SUN TZU, THE ART OF WAR

T HE FIRST ASSUMPTION from which we will attempt to break free is
that we can have good without bad. This assumption is so basic to
Western thought that we confuse it with truth, if we see it at all. In fact, it
is hard to imagine another view because all of our ambitions are founded
on the pursuit of good without evil.

Our Western upbringing has trained us to pursue good without bad,
health without sickness, happiness without sadness, strength without
weakness. We want profit without loss, growth without decline, and
strength without competition. Yet this ambition runs counter to the
Eastern way, in particular the principle of polarity, which says that bad
necessarily accompanies good (not judgements but two sides of the same
coin), and decline follows growth. Companies that embrace polarity
create options and goals that other companies do not have. They perplex
us with their ability to outmaneuver competitors, to lock-in consumers,
and control their environments. According to Yin Yang, we work with the
natural laws that bind good and bad to achieve a balance we prefer.

Instead of trying to dominate our markets by consistently beating our competition, we might seek a harmony with our opponents. From the Western perspective, this may seem impractical or weak; but in practice, it is neither. Polarity helped emperors navigate some of China's most turbulent and violent eras, the Spring and Autumn period (770–476 B.C.) when the centralized feudal system that had maintained relative calm disintegrated, and the Warring States period (475–221 B.C.) when forty-four feudal states battled each other for land, conquering each other until only seven kingdoms, all of roughly equal strength, remained. Constant, fluid contention in the forms of war and political gaming typified these periods. Out of this environment a philosopher named Lao Tzu (c. 551–479 B.C.) created the *Tao Te Ching* which, like Nicolo Machiavelli's *The Prince*, was meant to guide leaders to greatness. He wrote:

> Being and non-being create each other.
> Difficult and easy support each other.
> Long and short define each other.
> High and low depend on each other.
> Before and after follow each other.
> There the Master [one who understands the Tao]
> acts without doing anything
> and teaches without saying anything.
> Things arise and she lets them come;
> things disappear and she lets them go.
> She has but doesn't possess,
> acts but doesn't expect.

—LAO TZU, *TAO TE CHING*, CHAPTER 2

The polarity principle does not imply complacent acceptance. On the contrary, it is an alternative way to achieve our ambitions. Lao Tzu argues that in working with, rather than against, the laws of nature—by accepting that everything is connected with its opposite—we can achieve our goals more quickly, with less energy, and our results will be more permanent.

The polarity principle has two key implications to business:

- We are usually better off seeking balance with, rather than trying to destroy, our competition
- We can better control our environment (e.g., our competitors, consumers, markets) by embracing the complex and interdependent nature of our situation

We should not always try to eliminate our competition. Indeed, we often need our competition in order to get ideas, to energize our workers, and to protect us against other competitors. We will see that fast-moving, aggressive companies like Microsoft, Virgin, and Coca-Cola benefit from their competitors.

When asked about the entry of Microsoft into the gaming business, Kazuo Hirai, president and chief operating officer of Sony Computer Entertainment America, said, "Am I worried? I was asked the same question six years ago about Nintendo and Sega. I think they have a lot to contribute to ensure the growth of the interactive entertainment sector. And if they bring a healthy dose of competition, it bodes well for the industry."[ii] This is the attitude of a company that embraces polarity.

Embracing the complexity of our environment reveals new strategic possibilities. We tend to cut problems into separate, more easily digested pieces to which we can apply logic and derive a solution. But this prevents us from seeing interesting relationships between players. Creative and competitive companies constantly play with relationships to squeeze out an advantage and profits.

The stratagems in this section help us to apply the polarity principle to our immediate situations. We will see that, while based on a philosophy fundamentally different from those of the West, polarity is regularly at work, helping the most successful Western companies gain advantage over their competitors, consumers, and allies.

> *Know how to use your enemies. Grasp things not by the blade, which will harm you, but by the hilt, which will defend you. The same applies to emulation. The wise person finds enemies more useful than the fool does friends.*
>
> —BALTASAR GRACIAN, *THE ART OF WORLDLY WISDOM*[iii]

To Catch Something, First Let It Go

欲擒故縱

Press the enemy force too hard and they will strike back fiercely.
Let them go and their morale will sink. Follow them closely, but do not
push them too hard. Tire them and sap their morale. Then you will be
able to capture them without shedding blood. In short, a careful
delay in attack will help bring victory.

—FROM *THE 36 STRATAGEMS*

W̲E ARE USUALLY better off letting an opponent escape. Trying to beat a surrounded opponent is costly in time, money, or lives, because the opponent, having less to lose, will fight more fiercely. A victory so won also is less permanent. A defeated opponent will look for revenge, but one that submits voluntarily can become useful.

KEY ELEMENTS:

- You "capture" your enemy

- Though you are able, you do not kill your enemy

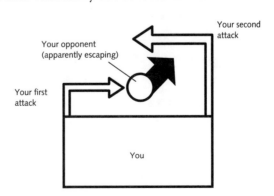

This stratagem points out two truths:

- Dominating your opponent often requires more energy than it is worth
- Force can win hands but rarely hearts

> *A prince ought to inspire fear in such a way that, if he does not win love,*
> *he avoids hatred; because he can endure very well being feared whilst he*
> *is not hated . . .*

—NICOLO MACHIAVELLI, *THE PRINCE*, CHAPTER 17[iv]

TO CAPTURE A COMPETITOR, LET IT GO   One of the most recounted corporate rivalries in history is that between Coca-Cola and Pepsi. It began just before the turn of the twentieth century and continues to occupy the time of MBA students in the top business schools today. What is strange about this rivalry is that is different from what we normally think of as a rivalry. It is war that neither company would want to win. The dynamic balance that Coca-Cola and Pepsi have struck exemplifies the polarity principle in action.

In 1886 a pharmacist in Georgia created Coca-Cola's formula, and a few years later Coca-Cola was introduced as a branded beverage to the public. In a move that would define the hundred-years' dance between these rivals, Pepsi-Cola followed seven years later. In 1893 a pharmacist from North Carolina invented the Pepsi formula and soon thereafter Pepsi implemented Coca-Cola's franchise-based business model. By 1910 Coca-Cola had 370 franchises to Pepsi's 270.

The consistency of the competitive pattern between Coca-Cola and Pepsi is astounding: A innovates, B copies, B innovates, A copies. While each company strives to create a unique advantage in the form of a new product, a new business model, or a new channel, it simultaneously tracks its adversary's efforts so that it can quickly follow. At the same time, each is trying to be different by innovating and the same by copying. Looking at the major events over just a ten-year span reveals the pace of this pattern:

INNOVATION	COPY
1980—Coca-Cola switches from using sugar in its cola to lower-priced high-fructose corn syrup	Pepsi follows suit three years later
1984—Pepsi switches from saccharine to aspartame to sweeten its diet product	Coca-Cola switches to aspartame six months later
1984—Pepsi introduces a two-liter bottle	Coca-Cola introduces its own two-liter bottle four months later
1985—Seven-Up runs a successful advertising campaign extolling the virtues of being caffeine-free	Coca-Cola and Pepsi launch caffeine-free versions of their own products that same year

Although they consider each other enemies, they are better off having each other. Without Pepsi, Coca-Cola might not be using saccharine or two-liter bottles. Without Coca-Cola, sugar might be cutting into Pepsi's margins, because Pepsi had never switched to high-fructose corn syrup. As Roger Enrico said in 1988 when he was CEO of Pepsi,

> The warfare must be perceived as a continuing battle without blood. Without Coke, Pepsi would have a tough time being an original and lively competitor. The more successful they are, the sharper we have to be. If the Coca-Cola Company didn't exist, we'd pray for someone to invent them.[v]

Coca-Cola and Pepsi play cat and mouse with each other, following closely, but never falling too far behind. When one lurches forward, the next pounces. But the pounces are never fatal. We can debate intentions, but the outcome is clear: Over one hundred years, Coca-Cola and Pepsi have spurred each other toward greatness without either company "winning."

> *When the opposition withdraws, never interfere;*
> *When surrounding the opposition, leave an opening;*

When the opponent is desperate, never press.
Such is the execution of Artful Strategy.

—SUN TZU, *THE ART OF WAR*[vi]

TO CAPTURE A HEART, LET IT GO SEVEN TIMES In A.D. 225, three kingdoms ruled China. One of these, Shu, had been trying unsuccessfully for years to force a group of tribes in its southern region into submission. The Shu ruler instructed an advisor, Zhuge Liang, to resolve the problem.

Zhuge Liang, with his superior military power, could have forced a decisive victory over the renegade tribes. But he worried that such a victory would be costly and short-lived. The resentment it would generate would complicate efforts to rule the region. He decided instead to win the tribe members' hearts and set out to do so by implementing the stratagem *To catch something, first let it go*. He set his sights on the king of the southern tribes, Menghou. In the first battle between Menghou's tribal army and the Shu army, it became clear that the tribal army was no match for the well-trained and equipped Shu. The Shu captured all three of Menghou's generals. But rather than close in on victory, Zhuge Liang fed Menghou's generals well and released them. The generals, who expected to be executed, were naturally grateful.

In response, Menghou launched an attack himself, and through some deft maneuvering and trickery by the Shu army, was taken prisoner. But Zhuge Liang again acted strangely. Rather than imprisoning or executing Menghou, he simply asked Menghou to pledge allegiance to the Shu kingdom. Menghou refused, but promised that if he were captured a second time he would admit inferiority and submit to Shu rule. Zhuge Liang had Menghou untied, treated him to wine and good food and released him. When Shu officers asked Zhuge Liang why he did not execute Menghou to end the siege definitively, Zhuge Liang explained that he was trying to win the hearts of the southern tribes, not merely defeat its armies.

Menghou planned a second attack. His general, who earlier had been captured and released by Zhuge Liang, failed and almost lost his life as punishment. These two events—being released by the enemy and nearly killed by his own ruler—shifted the general's allegiance. He captured Menghou and presented him to Zhuge Liang. For a second time, Menghou was a prisoner of the Shu. For a second time, Zhuge Liang asked Menghou to submit. For a second time, Menghou declined. And for a second time, Zhuge Liang had Menghou untied, fed, and released. Menghou returned home, hunted down his general and had him executed.

Menghou then planned a third assault. This time, he had his brother, and a large entourage dressed as civilians, bring gifts to Zhuge Liang. Once inside Zhuge Liang's camp, this band prepared to take the Shu forces by surprise and capture Zhuge Liang. But Zhuge Liang anticipated

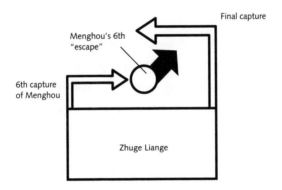

the trap. When the attack came, his men were prepared. They captured Menghou, who led the attack, but again Menghou refused to submit and again Zhuge Liang released him.

This back and forth continued four more times. In one instance, Menghou and his men fell into a trap laid by the Shu army. In another instance, a king loyal to Menghou turned on him, capturing and delivering him to Zhuge Liang. In yet another, Menghou and an entourage pretended to surrender, but when searched were revealed to be carrying daggers and swords with which they planned to kill Zhuge Liang. Each time Menghou was asked to submit, he refused and was released.

After the sixth capture, few Menghou supporters remained. Menghou mounted a seventh attack on a Shu outfit. The outfit played a game of cat and mouse for two weeks, setting up camp, pretending to retreat, and setting up camp again. In the last move of this pursuit, Menghou's army found itself trapped in a valley. Most of the army died. Menghou found himself captured for the seventh time. By now Menghou, with little support or morale, submitted to Zhuge Liang and to Shu rule of his tribes.

Zhuge Liang rewarded Menghou with a kingdom, land, and dominion over the southern tribes. When asked why he returned Menghou to power rather than put a Shu ruler in his place, Zhuge Liang explained that the people of southern tribes would be more loyal to Menghou than to a Chinese ruler and that by playing cat and mouse he had won Menghou's heart. The victory, therefore, was more stable.

> *Nothing in the world is more soft and yielding than water. Yet for dissolving the hard and inflexible, nothing can surpass it.*
> *The soft overcomes the hard, the gentle overcomes the rigid.*
> *Everyone knows this is true, but few can put it into practice.*

—LAO TZU, *TAO TE CHING*, CHAPTER 78[vii]

SUMMARY Most businesses in the West focus on beating their competition, but this assumes that we are better off without our competition. The polarity principle implies that optimal success depends on our competitor's success, or at least its continued existence.

Applying the polarity principle to competition reveals a model for competition that is very different from our traditional Western concept—a model in which competition is codependence, a dance, rather than a war. This model opens our thinking, and allows us to see new strategic possibilities. It encourages us to ask, "What if we do not actually want to beat our competition—what would we do differently?"

Applying the give and take of the polarity principle to value, as the next stratagem describes, can similarly liberate our thinking.

Exchange a Brick for a Jade

地磚引玉

Use a bait to lure the enemy and take him in.

—FROM *THE 36 STRATAGEMS*

O N THE SURFACE, *Exchange a brick for a jade* means simply to trade something of little value for something of more value, which may seem as wise and as useless as "buy low, sell high." But its deeper lesson has enabled companies like Microsoft, Sony, and Gillette to establish long-term control over their markets. The keys to its success rest on two human tendencies that Taoism and Buddhism attempt to eliminate:

- Value is relative. Yet we act as if only one value exists
- We confuse what we value with what others value

KEY ELEMENTS:

- You give your adversary something on which you place relatively little value

- In exchange, your adversary gives you something you value much more

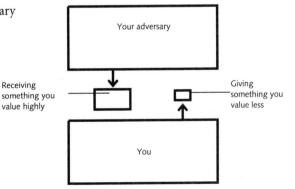

Your adversary

Receiving something you value highly

Giving something you value less

You

COMMITMENT AS A JADE Consumers often give up value because they have no way to measure or realize the value. Companies such as Microsoft and Sony have built their businesses to a great extent on spinning these consumer tendencies into profit.

When we consider buying a product, we judge its fair price by comparison to alternatives. If we're shopping for a video game console, for example, we might compare the price tag of, say, Sony's PlayStation 2 to that of Microsoft's Xbox. If no close substitutes exist we might try a more distant substitute as a comparison—comparing the price of the game console to the cost of seeing a movie every week for a year, for example.

Unfortunately for us, we exclude an important variable from our calculations: the full value the seller (i.e., Sony or Microsoft) realizes from establishing a relationship with us. This value is almost always higher than the profit the seller generates from the first sale. In other words, we often give up jades for bricks because we do not appreciate the worth of what we are trading. The jade we are giving up is dependence.

Sony is willing to lose $100–$150 on each PlayStation 2 it sells because with each sale it establishes a codependent relationship with a new consumer. This allows Sony to shift from a one-off relationship to a long-term one to which it can put polarity to work. It can manage this relationship to generate attractive, long-term profits—initially from software sales, but eventually from Internet services, movie rentals, and any number of yet-to-be-imagined products.

Of course, this strategy can be described as setting up or switching costs that hinder a consumer from buying software for competing systems. Polarity, accepting good with bad or short-term loss for long-term gain, is simply another way to view this strategy. And when we use polarity to explain Sony's strategy, Microsoft's abrupt decision to enter the video game business in 2000 becomes less puzzling.

Microsoft also relies heavily on *Exchange a brick for a jade*. Indeed, some argue that Microsoft's strategy is dictated as much by this principle as by its core product—software. Microsoft built its business by distributing DOS and Windows so widely that they became standards, thereby establishing millions of codependent relationships with computer makers and consumers. The resulting mass of relationships eventually resembled a monopoly position in the software sector. Microsoft's success comes from expanding and leveraging these relationships, not just from building better-performing software.

With this view, that Microsoft is built on relationships as much as on software competencies, we can appreciate why Microsoft felt threatened by Sony's plan to add Internet capability to its PlayStation 2 (announced in September 1999): Sony was about to steal many of Microsoft's relationships. This is why Microsoft, which had never taken the video game segment seriously and had never manufactured hardware, suddenly decided to do both. As Michael Ribero, an executive vice president of game publisher Midway Games Inc., said, "Game consoles can be a kind of Trojan horse in the living room. You start playing games and then eventually use the console for other entertainment or for e-commerce."

Microsoft reacted in the first half of 2000. It announced plans to enter the interactive gaming business with its own soon-to-be-developed console called Xbox. The Microsoft console differed in intriguing ways from others; for example, it had a hard drive. But Microsoft's strategy remained the same: *Exchange a brick for a jade.* Microsoft planned to invest $500 million in marketing the Xbox, and to lose about $125 on each unit it sold, with the aim of profiting on future sales to its consumers of games, Internet services, and e-commerce capabilities.

VALUE IS RELATIVE Chuang Tzu was a Taoist philosopher, a contemporary of Lao Tzu, known for his humorous and colorful stories. One of his favorite themes was that value is relative. In other words, what we consider good or bad, beautiful or ugly, valuable or worthless, does not exist in an absolute. Rather, it depends only on our point of view.

One of his stories centers around an old tree most people found worthless. It was so knotted that it offered not an inch of flat wood, making it useless to carpenters. It was so ugly that no painter wanted to paint it nor gardener to decorate it.

But the characteristics that made it worthless to carpenters, painters, and gardeners were considered quite the opposite by the tree itself. Indeed they saved the tree's life. Because no one saw value in cutting the tree down, it grew unharmed for hundreds of years. Chuang Tzu's lesson is that value depends on perspective. It is not absolute.

WE CONFUSE OUR VALUE WITH OTHERS' Another story, by an unknown author, describes an old monk who lived by himself in an ample but modest home. One evening a thief, believing the house empty, broke in. He found very little of value: some pots and some food. As he rustled around looking for something worth taking home, he was startled to find the monk quietly meditating in one of the rooms.

The monk greeted the thief and asked what he wanted. When the thief explained that he was there to rob whatever he could find of value, the monk apologized: "I am sorry you have gone through such trouble and I have nothing of worth to give you. Here, take my clothes. They will surely get you more money than those pots or that food." The thief took the clothes and left the house.

The monk, now naked, returned to his meditation. Looking out his window at the sky he thought, "I wish I could have given him the moon. It is so beautiful."

One lesson from this story (there are a few) is that outward measures of something's value blind us from its true worth. The thief was so entranced by the value of clothes that he could not appreciate the moon. Ironically, the thief had to steal the clothes but already "had" the moon in that he could use it to light his way home and enjoy its beauty. But because no market price for the moon existed he had no basis for valuing.

SUMMARY *Exchange a brick for a jade* is a simple but powerful concept that has delivered dominant positions to many leading companies:

- Sony dominates interactive games (53 percent of the market share for consoles)
- Microsoft dominates operating systems
- Gillette dominates razors (profiting from blades rather than razors)
- American Airlines revolutionized the airline industry by trading miles for loyalty (introducing the first frequent flier program)

All companies depend *on* consumers, but those that establish a similar dependency *by* consumers on the companies move these relationships into polarity. This unlocks the potential to generate attractive, long-term rents.

Two truths—(1) that value is relative (yours is unlikely to match mine) and (2) that we tend to confuse what we value with what others value—create opportunities for us to exchange bricks for jades to entice consumers into codependent relationships. [See Appendix A for brainstorming exercises.]

We can also entice competitors into dependency. The next stratagem shows that doing so enables companies to increase their competitiveness and even to turn disadvantage into advantage.

Invite Your Enemy Onto the Roof, Then Remove the Ladder

上屋抽梯

Expose your weak points deliberately to entice the enemy to penetrate into your line, then surround him by cutting off his exit.

—FROM *THE 36 STRATAGEMS*

STRATAGEM 1, *To catch something, first let it go,* warns against surrounding an enemy because a surrounded enemy is willing to fight to the death. This stratagem, *Invite your enemy onto the roof, then remove the ladder,* offers situations in which we should surround our opponent. In removing our ladder, we commit our people to victory, and we empower them to win. In removing our opponent's ladder, we prevent an escape, and we force our opponent to compete where we hold the advantage.

The "ladder" in this stratagem symbolizes a path of entry and escape. A ladder allows one to ascend the battleground and escape if necessary. Without an escape ladder we reach a state of clarity: We have only one choice—to survive we must succeed.

KEY ELEMENTS:

- You entice your adversary to enter your area of control
- You cut off your adversary's and your soldiers' escape routes
- This motivates your soldiers . . .
- . . . and disadvantages your adversary

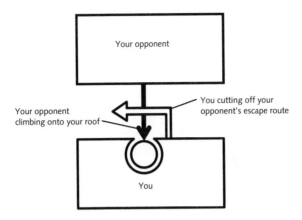

REMOVING OUR MANAGERS' LADDERS The first benefit of removing a ladder is that it motivates our soldiers or managers. Sun Tzu and Jack Welch, the former chairman and CEO of General Electric, both appreciated this.

In *The Art of War*, Sun Tzu counseled generals to use the motivational effect of commitment to their advantage:

> *At the critical moment, the leader of an army acts like one who has climbed up a height and then kicks away the ladder behind him. He carries his men deep into hostile territory before he shows his hand.*
> *The further you penetrate into a country, the greater will be the solidarity of your troops, and thus the defenders will not prevail against you.*[viii]

Mr. Welch used this tactic to transform of one of the world's largest corporations from a sleepy behemoth into an agile attacker. Before Mr. Welch became head of the company, GE's employees felt secure. Their "contract," as Mr. Welch called it, was that of lifetime employment: As long as they met average performance, their incomes were safe. As a result, managers felt little pressure to outperform.

Mr. Welch removed this safety ladder. He forced his managers to face competition:

Like many other large companies in the United states, Europe, and Japan, GE has had an implicit psychological contract based on perceived lifetime employment. . . .

The new psychological contract, if there is such a thing, is that jobs at GE are the best in the world for people who are willing to compete. We have the best training and development resources and an environment committed to providing opportunities for personal and profession growth.[ix]

Life under Mr. Welch was tough. But it also was rewarding for those who could compete. Mr. Welch rigorously measured managers' performance against operational metrics. He consistently demanded quarterly profit growth, and he linked managers' pay to company performance by issuing stock options. In 1980, when Mr. Welch took over, GE granted fewer than 1,000 employees stock options. By 2000, it granted stock options to more than 15,000 employees. Mr. Welch aggressively weeded out managers who could not thrive under this scrutiny. Despite numerous acquisitions, including RCA, GE cut its ranks by nearly 100,000 employees during Mr. Welch's twenty-year term.

MICROSOFT LURES BRITANNICA ONTO ITS ROOF In 1988, Encyclopedia Britannica was the world's leading English-language encyclopedia. Originally published in Scotland in 1768, it was also one of the oldest encyclopedias. Through 130 years of publishing, updating, and republishing, it built two seemingly insurmountable assets: credibility and deep content. These assets were key success factors in the encyclopedia business. Consumers, who had to invest more than $1,000 for a complete volume, demanded that the content be authoritative and exhaustive. These assets were also defendable. Any new competitor would have to invest in years of losses as it built and rebuilt content, slowly establishing its credibility, to catch up. Britannica's foundation seemed secure.

However, in that same year, 1988, Microsoft set its sights on the encyclopedia business. It hired a visual designer into the company's multi-media group to begin designing the "look" of a hypothetical electronic, multimedia, CD-based encyclopedia.

For five years Microsoft designed, built, and assembled the pieces of what it hoped would offer a superior value proposition to established encyclopedias. It borrowed credibility and content from *Funk & Wagnall's Encyclopedia* and added features that would differentiate its product from Britannica's:

- Searchability—users could search for information in multiple ways. In addition to the traditional alphabetical method, users could search by key-word and by category

- Multimedia—Microsoft's research showed that children learned more when presented with colorful pictures and moving images, so Microsoft included 800 full-color maps (with voice pronunciations, a "zoom" feature, and 100 historical maps), 100 animations, and seven hours of sound (including historic speeches, famous pieces of music, nature sounds, and foreign languages)

- More graphics—7,000 illustrations and photographs

- A 20-foot historical timeline—from 15 million B.C. to the present which allowed users to click on and explore historic events

- Thousands of cross-links—that enabled users to easily jump from one topic to a related one

- Greater timeliness—electronic content is easier to update than print (e.g., adding a paragraph does not require reformatting all subsequent pages, as is the case with actual books), so Microsoft could promise content would be more fresh

By the time Microsoft completed development of its encyclopedia, which it named *Encarta,* in 1993, Britannica's advantages appeared less impressive. To complete its list of advantages, Microsoft leveraged something Britannica could not: cost. It only cost about $1 to produce a CD. So Microsoft could, and did, price *Encarta* far below the cost of a set of Britannica books—at about $300 it was less than a third Britannica's cost. A reviewer wrote in the *Guardian*, "For less than the cost of a Britannica [book set], you can now buy a multimedia personal computer with CD-ROM drive and the leading electronic encyclopedias."[x] *Encarta* quickly became the top-selling educational CD.

Microsoft's aggressive pricing removed Britannica's ladder. Had Microsoft priced *Encarta* in line with a set of Britannica books, its value proposition might have been sufficiently comparable that the two products could have coexisted. Consumers who wanted in-depth content would buy books, and those who wanted multimedia would buy *Encarta*. But by pricing *Encarta* at $300, Microsoft left little choice for Britannica but to follow suit. Britannica had to cross the river to Microsoft's shore because its riverbank was eroding. How long would consumers be willing to pay so much more for a product with clear disadvantages?

Britannica responded two years later. But when it did, it stumbled, because it was forced to rush into a business it did not understand, and because it was playing by rules that gave Microsoft the advantage.

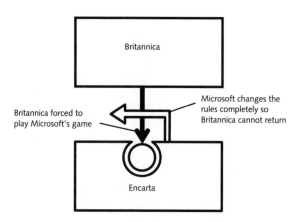

Britannica introduced its CD product in 1995, but because the company did not have the skills or time—it took Microsoft five years to develop *Encarta* while Britannica had less than two—the first Britannica

CD was little more than Britannica text in electronic form. The company hoped its superior brand name and content depth would compensate for a lack of multimedia.

Consumers might have accepted this proposition had Britannica not committed a fatal pricing error. Perhaps because it did not understand the CD-ROM market or, more likely, because it wanted to prevent cannibalization of its core product, Britannica priced its CD product at $1,000—three times the price of Encarta. Sales were, naturally, unimpressive.

Finally, in 1997, after two years in the market, Britannica accepted its new reality and began playing by the new rules. It slashed its price to match competition at $125 and added web links and multimedia content to its latest release.

Britannica had better, but still spotty success online. It was the first to offer an online service, www.eb.com, which offered users, for a fee, access to Britannica's thirty-two volumes of content. The site switched fee structures a few times, and in 1999 Britannica decided try an advertising-based model. It created Britannica.com to offer users full access to Britannica's volumes at no cost. The site was so popular that it crashed and was down for three weeks.

Before 1993, *Britannica* was the leading encyclopedia, with impressive sources of strategic advantage and 250 years of experience. Yet in just a few years' time a new brand nearly toppled this institution. It did so not by force, nor by direct competition. Rather, it invited Britannica onto its roof, where multimedia skills rather than heritage determined success, and then removed the ladder. Britannica could no longer return to its old world where credibility and deep content alone guaranteed success.

As we see in the Microsoft-Britannica example, by removing our enemy's ladder we can force her to compete where we hold the advantage. This is risky. Our adversary can become desperate and difficult to beat. But if applied in the right situation, as the following story shows, it can provide a steady foundation for victory.

REMOVING YOUR ENEMY'S LADDER In 206 B.C. the Han kingdom unified China. During the subsequent Han dynasty, which lasted over 400 years to A.D. 220, China experienced a renaissance that included the revival of Confucianism, the invention of paper (a thousand years before paper appeared in the West) and the writing of the first dictionaries and general histories of China. This renaissance owes much to the Han's martial capabilities and adept use of stratagems. The Han ruled by force, regularly attacking rebel kingdoms to keep them under the Han fold.

In one such instance a famous Han general, Han Xin, traveled to quell two revolts. While he was on his way, a third kingdom attempted to stop him. When Han Xin reached the Wei River he found an army of 200,000 soldiers ready to battle him on the other side. Han Xin appeared to have three choices, none attractive: He could attack; but his solders, wading through water toward an enemy on solid ground, would be at a severe disadvantage and likely lose their lives. He could return home; but in failing his emperor, he might lose his own life. He could wait; but his opponent had no reason to attack nor to leave. Han Xin would not reach the revolts in time and still would fail his emperor.

So Han Xin applied the stratagem *Invite your enemy onto the roof, then remove the ladder*. He ordered his solders to dam the river upstream with sandbags. As night fell, so did the water level. In the morning, Han

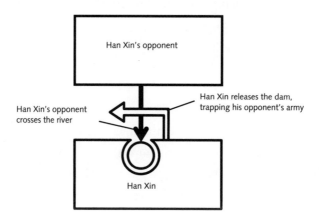

Xin attacked. His solders easily crossed the shallow river. Their opponent was prepared but no longer held a clear advantage.

Soon after the two armies engaged, Han Xin ordered his soldiers to retreat. The opposing general sensed that Han Xin was about to fall and ordered his troops to follow. When half the opposing army had crossed the dry river, Han Xin ordered his soldiers, who had been hiding near the dam, to quickly dismantle it. Pent-up waters crashed down on and drowned the half of the opposing army still in the river's path. In one move Han Xin had done the following:

- Cut his opponent's size in half (from 200,000 to 100,000 soldiers)
- Obtained the advantage of terrain (he was now on high ground with freedom of movement, while his opponent was on low ground and restricted by a river)
- Shifted from attacker to defender

Han Xin used *Invite your enemy onto the roof, then remove the ladder* to manipulate his attackers into a precarious position and then defeat them with minimal loss of his own soldiers' lives.

Strategically creative corporations use a maneuver similar to Han Xin's to win markets. By luring a competitor out of his market and into our own, and doing this in such a way that the competitor cannot return, we can quickly change the rules of competition in our favor to topple even a more powerful incumbent. Microsoft's entry into encyclopedias illustrates this clearly.

SUMMARY We have considered dancing with our competitors (*To catch something, first let it go*). Why not also consider embracing them firmly? Invite our competitors to compete directly with us. This can drive our managers to higher levels of performance and can potentially switch the rules of competition into our favor. Who, after all, is better suited to compete on your roof than you?

Lure the Tiger Down from the Mountain

調虎離山

Use unfavorable natural conditions to trap the enemy in a difficult position. Use deception to lure him out. In an offensive that involves great risk, lure the enemy to come out against you.

—FROM *THE 36 STRATAGEMS*

A PERMUTATION OF the tactic *Invite your enemy onto the roof, then remove the ladder* is to lure your adversary out of a stronghold and onto neutral territory. Both tactics advise inducing your adversary to leave the area where he or she holds an advantage, but the second does not advise inviting your adversary into your territory. Rather, by pulling your adversary to terrain on which you are equally competitive, you benefit in three ways:

- You even your odds of success by removing your competitor's advantage
- Your competitor exposes a stronghold to attack by leaving it
- You leave open an exit for retreat

The tiger, which is indigenous to the mountains, is difficult to hunt in her natural terrain. By luring her out of the mountain, onto the open field where you each have an equal chance of winning, you remove the advantage and put her stronghold at risk.

KEY ELEMENTS:

- Your adversary is in a stronghold

- You lure your adversary out of this stronghold

- You either (1) attack on open ground or (2) attack the stronghold

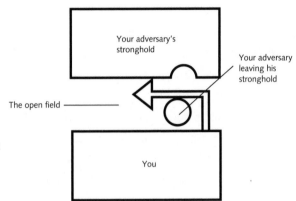

LURING HÄAGEN-DAZS ONTO THE FIELD OF FLAVOR In the early 1990s, the ice cream company Ben and Jerry's temporarily lured Häagen-Dazs out of its stronghold and damaged Häagen-Dazs as a result.

Ben and Jerry's eroded Häagen-Dazs's dominant position in the superpremium ice cream segment by offering unconventional flavors and names. Although it was losing overall market share, Häagen-Dazs remained the ultimate ice cream maker. It retained a loyal base of customers who chose the company's products for consistent high-quality ice cream. Ben and Jerry's off-the-wall approach could not lure away Häagen-Dazs's core consumers.

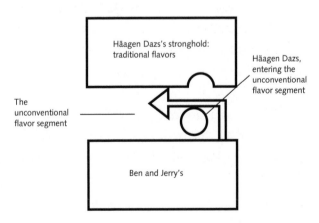

But after Ben and Jerry's captured 29 percent of the superpremium ice cream market, Häagen-Dazs decided to defend more aggressively. It came out of its stronghold to attack Ben and Jerry's directly. It introduced unconventional flavors, such as Carrot Cake Passion, Cappuccino Commotion, Caramel Cone Explosion, Triple Brownie Overload, and Peanut Butter Burst.

The results were poor—but not because Häagen-Dasz could not compete in this unconventional flavor segment. Indeed, because Ben and Jerry's was still a young brand, one might have reasonably expected Häagen-Dazs to develop a viable unconventional flavor business. Rather, in straying from traditional flavors, Häagen-Dazs weakened its stronghold by confusing its core customers and therefore damaging its brand identity. This brand cost came with little benefit. Häagen-Dazs could not even steal significant market share from Ben and Jerry's as a payoff. Häagen-Dazs was caught out of its stronghold and risked losing its stronghold as a result.

A TIGER LOSES HER MOUNTAIN   Toward the end of the Han dynasty (221 B.C.–A.D. 220), China's warlords had consolidated power such that only a few independent states remained. South of the Yangtze River two rivals emerged: Sun Ce and Liu Xun. They eyed each other carefully. Whichever one survived their pending confrontation would rule all of southern China.

Liu Xun's capital was difficult to attack. It was well fortified, surrounded by mountains, reachable by only a few narrow routes, each of which he could easily defend. Sun Ce had little hope of taking Liu Xun directly so he and his advisors devised a plan to lure Liu Xun down from his mountain.

In A.D. 199, Sun Ce sent an emissary to Liu Xun. This emissary carried precious gifts and a letter. In the letter, Sun Ce praised Liu Xun for his military might and acknowledged Sun Ce's own inferiority. Liu Xun was pleased by the words.

In the letter, Sun Ce went on to complain about another state,

Shangliao, that regularly attacked his territory. Shangliao, he explained, although small, was too large for Sun Ce to handle alone. He proposed that Liu Xun attack Shangliao with Sun Ce providing reinforcements. This, he argued, would offer three benefits: Victory would be assured because Liu Xun's powerful forces reinforced with Sun Ce's smaller army would overpower their enemy. The victory would deliver Liu Xun great wealth, because Shangliao was rich. And in the process, Liu Xun would expand his territory, becoming even more powerful.

Liu Xun was intrigued by the proposal. He consulted his advisors, one of whom argued against the plan. This advisor did not trust Sun Ce. He pointed out that defeating Shangliao would be difficult and nearly impossible if Sun Ce failed to provide reinforcements. He warned that if Liu Xun left his stronghold with his army, the stronghold would lie vulnerable. Sun Ce might attack it.

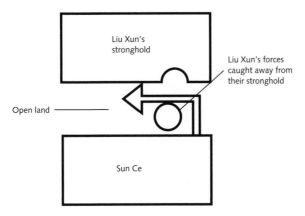

But Liu Xun, hungry for wealth and power, ignored this advice. He ordered his generals to prepare for battle.

Liu Xun's forces marched to Shangliao and surrounded the city. Tired from travel, they were unprepared for the vigorous defense the city's army had prepared. Complicating their situation even further, Sun Ce's reinforcements never appeared. Arrows rained down from the city, cutting down Liu Xun's forces. Their siege failed.

Meanwhile, Sun Ce learned of Liu Xun's expedition and ordered his troops into action—not to support Liu Xun but to attack his stronghold. Lui Xun had left behind only a small secondary force, which Sun Ce easily overpowered.

When Liu Xun returned with his soldiers, defeated, tired, and now demoralized they found their home conquered by Sun Ce. They did not have the energy to take back their city. After some effort, they surrendered. The tiger was unable to return to her mountain.

SUMMARY Our competitor is skilled at playing his game in his market. Competing with him head-on may be a costly, high-risk strategy. But we even the odds, possibly even reverse them, by switching the playing field. The tiger is caught more easily on the open field.

Befriend the Distant Enemy
to Attack One Nearby

遠交近攻

It is more advantageous to conquer nearby enemies, because of
geographical reasons, than those far away. So ally yourself temporarily
with your distant enemies in spite of political differences.

—FROM *THE 36 STRATAGEMS*

WE LIKE TO DRAW clear lines between supporters and competitors. But it is becoming difficult to do so. This stratagem shows that by simply selecting the right supporters and targeting the right competitors, we can play one off the other and become more powerful.

When companies defined themselves by industry, identifying competitors was straightforward: If a company played in our industry it was a competitor; otherwise, it was not. Now lines are blurring. Companies increasingly define their businesses along dimensions that cross industries. Few thought Microsoft would feel threatened by Sony's PlayStation, for example, or that Virgin, a record company, would threaten British Airways, as we shall see later. While companies in unrelated industries are finding themselves unexpected rivals, other companies in the same industry increasingly find themselves allies. Identifying the right competitors and the right allies is becoming more complicated and a more important determinant of success.

This stratagem offers some advice for navigating a web of alliances: Ally with competitors that are more "distant" from you and attack competitors that are "nearer" to you.

KEY ELEMENTS:

- You ally with a distant enemy

- You attack a nearby enemy

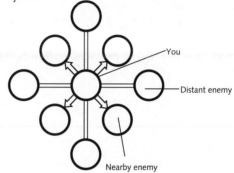

CONSOLE MANUFACTURERS BEFRIEND GAME DEVELOPERS Opportunities to ally with "distant" competitors abound. We can find areas of common interest among even our most direct rivals. Video game console makers and independent game developers, for example, should be direct rivals by most measures. Yet they have established a balance between competition and cooperation that makes them both better off.

Video game console makers (Sony, Nintendo, and Microsoft, etc.) develops their own games through internal divisions or wholly owned development companies. They like to sell their own games. They make higher profits margins on them: generally 50–70 percent, or $25–$35, as compared to just 10 percent, or $5–$10, on games developed by third parties. So why do console makers sell independently developed games at all?

Console makers could probably put independent developers out of business if they wanted, because they control access to consumers. Contracts between independent developers and console makers usually give console makers exclusive rights to manufacture the game and distribute it to retailers. If the console maker hits production snags, or fails to fully distribute a new product, developers have little recourse. Console makers can even require developers to prepay part of their manufacturing costs.

Yet, console makers and independent developers coexist because they are "distant enemies" for three reasons: Software success is unpredictable, a diversity of games is important, and the makers and developers have purposely aligned their incentives. The game software business, like most entertainment businesses, is characterized by erratic product success. Predicting what will make a "hit" with consumers or what they will turn their backs on is difficult. To cast a wide net, console makers try to maximize the number of games available for their hardware. So they simultaneously develop their own games and actively court third-party developers. Microsoft, for example, went to great lengths to build excitement for Xbox among developers by involving them in Xbox's design process, and by delivering development kits (software and hardware that enable developers to create new games) earlier than its competitors.

Having lots of games also attracts new users. So console makers like to have independent developers develop games for their hardware, even if they make much less profit.

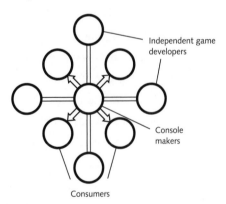

Independent game developers

Console makers

Consumers

The third reason that console makers and independent game developers are "distant enemies" is that their economic incentives are aligned. As described in *Exchange a brick for a jade*, console makers lose money on each console sold. This aligns their incentives with those of game developers. The economics of console development and software development are similar: Developers sink a significant investment in developing a game (anywhere from $1 million to $5 million[xi]) with the hope of recouping the investment through wide distribution of the completed product. Software developers and console makers therefore both want to get as many consoles as possible into consumers' homes.

This is why when Microsoft decided to enter the game business, it did something it had never done before: manufacture computers. Because success requires befriending game developers and aligning incentives, it means losing money on consoles to earn it back on software. Microsoft could not find a company to produce Xboxes independently. As J. Allard, General Manager for the Xbox platform, said, "We talked to Michael Dell, and the guys at Gateway and Compaq. They said, 'Wait, you want to make 50 million of the same exact thing? That's not what we do.' Dell said, 'I don't want to be in the razor business if I can't get in on the blades. You're talking to the wrong guy.' "[xii]

Aligning incentives with game developers is essential. Had Microsoft stuck with its old model of developing software to run on other people's hardware, it would likely have suffered the same fate of a gaming company called 3DO. Founded in 1990 as a console maker named Medio, 3DO's model depended on both hardware and software being profitable. Over seven years, 3DO grew rapidly; it went public in 1993. But it eventually hit an obstacle: It could not convince developers to make games for its platform. 3DO's hardware manufacturers had only one source of profit: console sales. So they demanded consoles remain profitable and had no reason to follow when Nintendo and Sega dropped prices below profitable levels. Game developers, who prefer to develop games for the platform with the largest consumer base, switched their efforts to developing games for Nintendo and Sega.

3DO's model fell apart. In 1997, 3DO exited the console business altogether to focus exclusively on development.

UNIFYING CHINA BY BEFRIENDING DISTANT ENEMIES During the Warring States period, China consisted of seven kingdoms, each pursuing dominance over the known world. Their contentious balance lasted for 250 years until Qin, one of the largest states, upset it. Qin ultimately enveloped the other kingdoms and unified China by acting on the principle *Befriend the distant enemy to attack one nearby.*

An advisor of the Qin emperor encouraged him to attack a state that, while quite distant for Qin, was weak and therefore easy prey. The emperor found this advice sound, and was ready to act when another advisor warned he should do the opposite. The advisor argued that Qin should not attack the smaller state because other large states, threatened by Qin's expansion, would come to the target state's defense. Indeed, the states nearby to Qin had already entered an alliance to defend themselves. The advisor also noted that attacking and ruling a distant state would require more resources and introduce more logistical problems than would attacking and ruling a neighbor.

Instead, the advisor suggested seeking alliances with distant states to attack neighboring ones. This strategy would have two key benefits: Qin would be the primary benefactor of these alliances because each nearby state, once taken, would naturally fall under the control of the larger partner, Qin. And such alliances would put outlying states off their guard by calming their fears of being future Qin targets (which, of course, they were). This would make conquering neighboring states easier, because

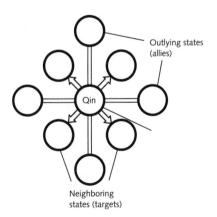

Outlying states
(allies)

Qin

Neighboring
states (targets)

outlying states would not come to their defense. It also would allow Qin to take the outlying states by surprise later.

The king followed this advice. He befriended distant states to attacked the ones nearby. This disrupted the natural alliance Qin might have otherwise encountered and paved the way for Qin to take over the entire country. For the first time in history, China was unified. Qin was its ruler.

SUMMARY We increasingly find allies among competitors, and competitors among seemingly unrelated companies. This creates opportunities. We can look for—even create—"distant" enemies to achieve common goals (attacking "nearby" enemies). By throwing away our automatic notions of friend and foe, new opportunities emerge.

Kill with a Borrowed Knife

借刀殺人

Your enemy's situation is clear but your ally's stand is uncertain.
At this time, induce your ally to attack your enemy in order to preserve your
strength. In dialectic terms, another man's loss is your gain.

—FROM *THE 36 STRATAGEMS*

INDIRECT ATTACKS ON your adversary are more likely to catch opponents off guard. When an indirect attack comes from a third party rather than from us, its effectiveness multiplies. This stratagem contemplates having someone else attack our adversary. Even if our adversary looks in the right direction, she is likely to look to the wrong person and so still fail to see our approach.

The most obvious application of this stratagem to business is to have one competitor attack another. Companies do this often. But we can find useful "borrowed knives" across our industries' value chains. Here we will see how one company successfully wielded a "borrowed knife" up its value chain, among suppliers, to establish a bargaining position and lock-in new profits.

KEY ELEMENTS:

- You induce a third party to attack your enemy

- You take no direct action

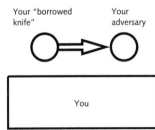

- You influence your adversary with a third party

BORROW YOUR ADVERSARY'S FOE Our adversaries' adversaries are often our friends. In a case made famous by Adam Brandenburger and Barry Nalebuff, Coca-Cola showed this to be true. Coca-Cola attacked its adversary by manipulating a competitor.

In the mid-1980s, Coca-Cola and Pepsi had been using the NutraSweet brand of the chemical aspartame to sweeten their diet products. They used the same brand of sweetener because the supplier, Monsanto, held a patent on aspartame production. However, this patent would soon expire—in 1987 in Europe and in 1992 in the United States.

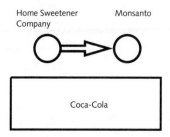

Once the patent expired, Coca-Cola and Pepsi potentially could switch suppliers. This clearly would lower costs. But both beverage companies had good reason to stay with Monsanto: Whoever switched suppliers would have to remove the NutraSweet brand from its can. If Pepsi did this and Coca-Cola did not, Pepsi would lose consumers to Coca-Cola. If Coca-Cola did this and Pepsi did not, Coca-Cola would lose consumers to Pepsi. In other words, unless someone upset the balance, neither drink company would switch. And because neither beverage company would switch, no new competitor would have reason to enter the aspartame market. The economics of entering the aspartame market without the possibility of gaining one of the two largest accounts were unattractive. Monsanto's hold appeared firm.

To free itself from this apparent trap, Coca-Cola borrowed a knife: a new aspartame producer. It encouraged the Home Sweetener Company to develop an aspartame business to compete with Monsanto once Monsanto's patents expired. The Home Sweetener Company, betting that Coca-Cola would become a customer, built capacity in Europe in 1995, two years before Monsanto's patent was due to expire there. It then developed plans to build capacity in the United States.

For the first time, Monsanto faced a genuine threat. Before the Home Sweetener Company existed, any threat by Coca-Cola to switch suppliers was impossible. Now such a threat was merely impractical. Before Monsanto's patents expired, and before the Home Sweetener Company could begin selling aspartame, Coca-Cola and Pepsi used their newfound leverage to negotiate long-term, low-price contracts with Monsanto, effectively killing the Home Sweetener Company's chances of survival. It is unlikely that Coca-Cola or Pepsi ever intended to award the Home Sweetener Company aspartame contracts. The company was a pawn—a borrowed knife.

Coca-Cola's maneuver illustrates one application of the stratagem *Kill with a borrowed knife.* It borrowed a supplier's competitor to attack a supplier. But the stratagem's applications are diverse. Each agent whose actions influence our success is a potential target for this stratagem. Take consumers as an example: By borrowing one consumer to market to another, we can propagate the reinforcing effects of "buzz marketing." Or consider the government: By borrowing regulators (e.g., through lobbying), we change the rules of the game to our advantage. The list of potential targets is unlimited.

TWO PEACHES The origin of the term "borrowed knife" is unknown. But a story from the Spring and Autumn period (770–476 B.C.) helps illustrate its essence.

A duke in the state of Qi was concerned. He and his state owed much of their prosperity to the three knights whose abilities and strengths had delivered many victories over the years. Stories of the knights' exploits had propelled them to hero status. And the duke, though grateful for the knights' contributions, was concerned by the knights' growing power.

When the knights showed signs of disobedience, failing to salute a high-ranking government official, for example, the duke decided to take preemptive action and have the knights killed.

For political and practical reasons, however, the duke could not act directly against the knights. What soldiers would have the will and courage to confront the state's most capable warriors? And if the soldiers somehow succeeded, how would the duke manage the popular reaction? The duke needed to borrow a knife, and he chose knives that had never failed him before—the knights themselves.

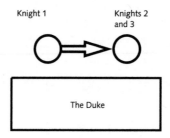

He wrapped two peaches in a gift box and anonymously sent them to the knights with a note that read, "He who has performed the greatest deeds may take a peach." The knights opened the gift and read the note. Then two knights each grabbed and ate a peach, each believing his deeds to be the greatest.

The third knight looked up from the now empty fruit basket and stared furiously at his colleagues. He called them liars. He accused them of greed and conceit, of breaking their code. He reprimanded them so severely that they took their lives.

When the remaining knight's rage subsided, he came to terms with the finality of his words. He had killed his two most dear companions over meaningless pride. His sense of guilt eventually drove him to suicide. The duke was free and his hands were clean.

SUMMARY Using a third party to attack our adversary may be more efficient than us attacking directly, and it may require fewer resources. It may also be more effective as it may catch our adversary off guard. Before we commit resources to direct action, we should think about borrowing a knife.

Consider the obvious choices (a competitor, a customer, the government, a supplier, etc.), but do not stop there. Only your imagination limits your options.

Besiege Wei to Rescue Zhao

圍魏救趙

It is wiser to launch an attack against the enemy force when
they are dispersed than to fight them when they are concentrated.
He who strikes first fails and he who strikes late prevails.

—FROM *THE 36 STRATAGEMS*

BESIEGE WEI TO RESCUE ZHAO, the tactic of coordinating your attack with that of an ally so as to force your adversary to battle on two fronts, can turn the table of fortune. It can help a weak army steal victory from the jaws of an entrenched defender. It can arm a small, young company with an advantage even in the face of a long-established leader. It can build global brands where none could exist before.

KEY ELEMENTS:

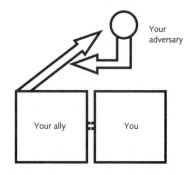

- You are in direct conflict with an adversary

- An ally of yours attacks your adversary

- Your adversary disengages from its conflict with you to defend itself

- Your adversary must now fight on two fronts. This multiplies your chances of success

VIRGIN BESIEGES BRITISH AIRWAYS By 1984, numerous start-up airlines had failed in their attempts to challenge British Airways in the U.K. British Airways held near-monopolistic power that seemed to make competition futile. So when the Virgin Group launched Virgin Atlantic, most industry experts were incredulous.

Virgin faced numerous disadvantages. It had less money, capacity, political clout, and experience, and it had no control of the reservation system. Its defeat seemed inevitable.

But Virgin could place a piece on the game board that its predecessors never had. By putting its brand into play, Virgin introduced a powerful new ally. Virgin flustered British Airways and set a course for victory.

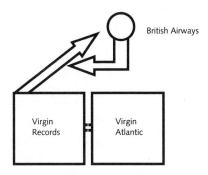

Because of its size and reputation, British Airways could deal with almost any direct competitor. But Virgin presented an enigma: It had already developed a strong brand in the music industry. Not only would British Airways have to deal with Virgin Atlantic, but it also would have to deal with Virgin Records. Each record Virgin Records sold helped win over passengers for Virgin Atlantic.

Virgin further complicated British Airways' position by expanding into the radio, television, and hotel businesses. British Airways, under attack from disparate directions, was unable to dispose of Virgin Atlantic with the ease it had put other start-up airlines out of business. In just five years Virgin Atlantic grew to £10 million in profits. And just five years later it expanded to Asia and Australia. Virgin learned that using one business to protect another rarely drains resources. Usually both businesses benefit. The stratagem *Besiege Wei to rescue Zhao* strengthens with use, as Richard Branson, the founder of the Virgin Group, observed:

> As well as protecting each other, they [the companies] have symbiotic relationships. When Virgin Atlantic starts a flight to South Africa, I find that we can launch Virgin Radio and Virgin Cola there. In the same way, we can use our experience in the airline industry to make buying train tickets easier and cheaper. We can draw on our experience of entertaining people on planes to entertain people on trains. We can use the cinemas to have people sample our Virgin Cola. We can use our vast stock of entertainment at the Virgin Megastores to make trips to Virgin Cinemas more fun.[xiii]

> *Appear at points which the enemy must hasten to defend; march swiftly to places where you are not expected.*
>
> —Sun Tzu, *The Art of War*[xiv]

STARBUCKS'S PERPETUAL SIEGE Until recently, the local coffee shop was a meeting place for coffee drinkers in the United States. Like the corner grocery store or tavern, the local coffee shop was a fixture and product of its neighborhood. Its brand extended no further than its home area. It only drew customers from within its neighborhood's borders and so did not compete with nearby coffee shops.

Today this landscape has shifted. The coffee shop is no longer a local phenomenon. Starbucks has trespassed on local coffee shops' neighborhoods, creating a chain that spreads across the U.S., into Europe, and even Asia. The company has injected new growth in the market, growing U.S. coffee shop revenues by 20 percent a year between 1997 and 2001. It has captured a disproportionate share of this expansion, growing its own revenues by 27 percent a year over the same period. Starbucks transformed the once sleepy, local-centric market into a high-growth market of national and international scope. It has done so by applying the principle of *Besiege Wei to rescue Zhao.*

To see Starbucks's method at work, imagine three neighborhood coffee shops in three neighborhoods equidistant from each other. These coffee shops do not compete with each other. The coffee, food, and ambience at each are equivalent, and the shops' locations do not bring these businesses into competition with each other because they are not in the same neighborhoods. A customer has no reason to travel out of her way to visit another coffee shop, so her neighborhood coffee shop is content.

Now imagine that one of the three coffee shops merges with another. These two sister coffee shops coordinate their operations. When one buys coffee, for example, it buys for two stores instead of one, and so buys at a lower price. And when it places an advertisement, it does so for two stores instead of one and thus can expect a larger return on its investment.

If the two coffee shops share the same name, even more advantages present themselves. By approaching customers on two fronts (i.e., customers see their same coffee shop name twice a day instead of just once), they can attract new customers into the market. This two-front attack also allows them to capture a larger share of the market: When one coffee shop wins a new customer, that customer becomes loyal to the sister shop as well and will be more willing to walk out of her way, even walk past a competing coffee shop, to visit the sister coffee shop whose name she recognizes. Loyal Starbucks customers, for example, will walk blocks to find a Starbucks. This loyalty cuts into the market share of competing

Local coffee shop battling Starbucks A *and* B

Starbucks A, winning loyalty

Starbucks B, ready to sell the customer coffee

neighborhood coffee shops (though in the case of Starbucks, neighborhood coffee shops often experience sales growth because overall market growth overcompensates for their market share losses).

The local coffee shop that once lived in relative balance with its competitors must now battle on two fronts. Similarly, customers who once were loyal to one coffee shop are now drawn to others on two fronts.

The outcome that results from applying this tactic is powerful. This stratagem gave both Starbucks and Wal-Mart seemingly unstoppable growth. Each company expanded only where its operations provided cover.

WHEN TWO PLUS TWO IS GREATER THAN ONE In 354 B.C. the Chinese state of Wei laid siege to its enemy, the state of Zhao. The weaker Zhao was unable to ward off its aggressor and appealed for help. Its hope lay in the hands of an ally, the state of Chi, which was led by a strong general named Tian and a wise strategist named Sun Bin.

General Tian assembled his troops and, together with Sun Bin, planned his strategy. They discussed their options. There were many to consider. Chi's army could supplement Zhao's in any number of ways, such as by fighting alongside Zhao's soldiers or by flanking Wei's solders. Each defensive option had its merits, but Sun Bin offered a superior tactic.

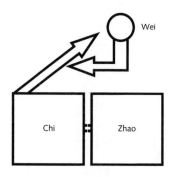

Since Wei's troops were at Zhao's doorstep, Wei's city was left exposed. Sun Bin calculated that by ignoring Wei's soldiers—indeed, by avoiding them entirely—Chi could both save Zhao and capture Wei. Although General Tian found Sun Bin's tactic unorthodox, Sun Bin had demonstrated his strategic skill many times before by using unorthodox tactics. General Tian accepted the plan and attacked the state of Wei directly.

Chi's attack on Wei forced Wei's army to abandon its siege of Zhao and to return home in its city's defense. But the journey home tired Wei's soldiers. They arrived unprepared, disorganized, and lacked the normal advantages of defense. As a result, Chi defeated them and saved Zhao in the process.

Like lions, which often attack in pairs to fluster their target, Chi and Zhao trapped Wei in an impossible dilemma. When implemented correctly, one plus one becomes greater than two.

summary The stratagem *Besiege Wei to rescue Zhao* advises using an ally or division to attack a competitor on two fronts. Even very different companies (e.g., a music retailer and an airline) may have enough in common to generate an advantage when properly coordinated. Using this stratagem can fluster an adversary and clear the way for seemingly unstoppable growth.

The Stratagem of
Sowing Discord

反間計

Use the enemy's spies to work for you and you will win
without any loss inflicted on your side.

—FROM *THE 36 STRATAGEMS*

CORPORATIONS ARE BUILT on relationships, from basic (with employees) to complex (e.g., with specialized outsourcers). Some argue that a corporation's core function is simply to aggregate and coordinate relationships. While these relationships are necessary for companies to specialize and grow, they also expose us to the risk that others will use them against us.

KEY ELEMENTS:

- You induce your adversary's agent to work in your favor

- You use this agent to topple a critical relationship on which your adversary depends

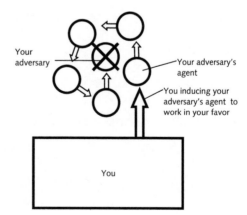

The enemy's spies who have come to spy on us must be sought out,
tempted with bribes, led away and comfortably housed. Thus they will
become converted spies and available for our service.

—SUN TZU, *THE ART OF WAR*, CHAPTER 13[xv]

COCA-COLA SOWS DISCORD IN VENEZUELA In 1996 Coca-Cola
outsold Pepsi in almost every market in the world. In Latin America,
Venezuela was the one country in which Pepsi enjoyed a lead. Venezuela
was a particular source of pride for Pepsi. Pepsi had outsold Coca-Cola
in the country for almost fifty years. Its sales were approaching four
times that of Coca-Cola's. But in August of that year Coca-Cola turned
this situation around overnight by applying *The stratagem of sowing*
discord.

Pepsi's Achilles' heel was Embotelladores Hit de Venezuela (EHV),
the sole Pepsi bottler and distributor in the country. Despite its long history, Pepsi's relationship with EHV was tenuous. Contrary to industry
practices, Pepsi held no equity in EHV. Previous requests by EHV for
additional investment from Pepsi went nowhere. So Coca-Cola
embarked on a campaign to achieve two things:

- To induce its adversary's agent (EHV) to work in its favor
- To use the relationship with EHV to topple Pepsi's dependence
  on EHV

Coca-Cola took aim at Pepsi's critical dependence. It entered into
secret talks with EHV aimed at convincing that company to switch its
allegiance. In late August 1996 Coca-Cola and EHV reached an agree-
ment under which Coca-Cola would buy 50 percent of EHV and invest
additional money into building its Venezuelan business. The talks were
so well hidden that Pepsi was taken by surprise upon hearing that a fifty-
year relationship had come to an abrupt end—that Pepsi's only bottler,
in the only Latin American country in which Pepsi held a lead, had suddenly switched sides.

Pepsi fought to hold on to its 45 percent market share. It said it would "exhaust all legal remedies in Venezuela and in the U.S."[xvi] It scrambled to find a new partner. But almost overnight, eighteen bottling plants switched over to Coca-Cola and 4,000 blue Pepsi trucks were painted over with Coca-Cola's red logo. Pepsi's market share dropped to almost zero, and Coca-Cola's 10 percent share shot up to 50 percent.

SOWING DISCORD IN CAO CAO'S CAMP During the Three Kingdoms period (A.D. 220–591), the warlord of Wei kingdom, a famous poet-turned-general named Cao Cao, was hunting down a rival warlord, Zhou Yu. Cao Cao was a powerful leader, a highly regarded strategist, and commanded a superior army to Zhou Yu's. His advantages were sound and he should have easily defeated Zhou Yu. But he had one critical dependence which Zhou Yu toppled using *The stratagem of sowing discord.*

Cao Cao grew up on the central plains of China. He and his army were unfamiliar with water and incompetent at waging war in it. Although they consistently routed Zhou Yu's army on dry land, their success ended at the rivers and riverbanks of a wetland area in which Zhou Yu had established his last defense.

Cao Cao had Zhou Yu cornered but was incapable of delivering the final blow. To turn this stalemate in his favor, Cao Cao hired two generals experienced in water-based warfare to train and lead his troops. In a short time, Cao Cao's men would learn enough about swimming through rivers and navigating marshes to complete their victory. The generals became Cao Cao's critical dependence. With them he would succeed. Without them success was unlikely.

While his men trained, Cao Cao decided simultaneously to pursue a diplomatic solution. One of his advisors happened to be an old friend of Zhou Yu. So Cao Cao ordered this advisor to visit the enemy and try to convince Zhou Yu to surrender.

The advisor, after trekking to Zhou Yu's camp, received a warm welcome from his old friend. Zhou Yu ordered a banquet served with large quantities of food, wine, and laughter. He refused to talk of politics, only old times, giving the advisor no opportunity to discuss surrender.

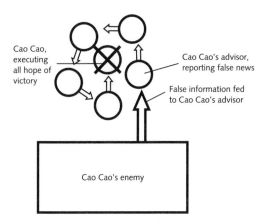

At the end of the night, Zhou Yu invited the advisor to sleep in his tent. The two settled into bed, closed their eyes, and calmed their breathing. But neither fell asleep. After some time the advisor, believing Zhou Yu actually had fallen asleep, and hoping to salvage something of his trip, quietly searched for something of value to bring back to Cao Cao.

He found a letter on Zhou Yu's desk with shocking information. The letter appeared to be from the two generals Cao Cao had hired to train his troops in water-based warfare. In the letter the generals affirmed their allegiance to Zhou Yu and their intentions to capture Cao Cao and sabotage his siege. The letter, of course, was a forgery planted by Zhou Yu to sow discord in Cao Cao's camp.

The next day the advisor reported the news to Cao Cao, who, infuriated, ordered the two generals executed. With them died Cao Cao's only chance of victory.

SUMMARY Viewing corporations as webs of relationships reveals interesting opportunities. Each relationship on which our adversary depends is a potential point of influence. By identifying our adversary's most critical relationships and, of those, determining the ones we can best influence, we uncover new tools for achieving our goals.

An interesting spin on this tactic is to play with relationships that do not directly influence our adversary, but rather influence how our adversary perceives her options. This indirectly influences her actions. The next stratagem, *Trouble the water to catch the fish*, explains this concept.

Trouble the Water to Catch the Fish

混水摸魚

*When the enemy falls into internal chaos, exploit his weakened
position and lack of direction and win him over to your side. This is
as natural as people going to bed at the end of the day.*

—FROM *THE 36 STRATAGEMS*

I T IS DIFFICULT to catch a fish with our bare hands because it reacts
quickly to our approach. But if we stir up the water around the fish so
that it becomes clouded with mud, the fish will not see our hand and will
be slow to react. We can then catch the fish more easily.

Companies use this principle to catch consumers. They intentionally
link seemingly unrelated products, or decouple products that normally
belong together, to change how customers perceive their options and
thereby the values of products they are considering.

KEY ELEMENTS:

- You create confusion
  around your adversary

- This blinds your
  adversary and so
  hinders his ability
  to understand your
  intentions or see
  your approach

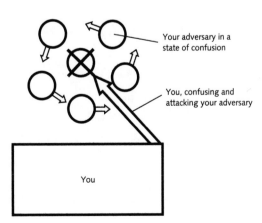

Your adversary in a
state of confusion

You, confusing and
attacking your adversary

You

When two fish are locked together in battle you can get both by catching just one.

—*CHINESE PROVERB*

"CONFUSING" THE CONSUMER By linking or decoupling products, marketers stir the water around customers to influence consumer's perception of value. This allows them to charge more for a product than a consumer would pay if she could measure what she was buying with clarity.

Consider Microsoft PowerPoint. It is today the leading presentation software in the world. It has grown so popular that many consumers forget that PowerPoint was a follower to Harvard Graphics. As Microsoft has done many times (e.g., in the encyclopedia business), it grew from a weak position, to oust an established leader, and dominate a new market. In this case Microsoft's success rested in a great part on troubling the water around Harvard Graphics consumers.

As Adam Brandenburger and Barry Nalebuff describe in *Coopetition,* Microsoft bundled its PowerPoint product with other products to confuse consumers trying to value the product. Microsoft made significant advances on PowerPoint that brought the program's performance in line with that of Harvard Graphics. To cut into Harvard Graphics' market, Microsoft could have sold its new PowerPoint version for significantly less than the $290 that Harvard Graphics charged. But if they did this, consumers might perceive PowerPoint to be inferior. So, instead, Microsoft kept the stand-alone price of PowerPoint high ($399) but bundled it with Word and Excel in its Office suite. Consumers believed they were getting a $399 program (PowerPoint) for free when they purchased Office. This pushed PowerPoint into the lead position.

We can also stir the water around consumers by taking the opposite approach: decoupling products. Financial institutions, for example, have found attractive profits in decoupling financial products. A bank can, for example, split the cash flow of a foreign bond into separate pieces: the principle payments, the interest payments, the cash flow related to foreign currency movements, etc. Although customers know how to value a complete foreign bond, for example, they have much greater difficulty valuing its pieces because the cash flows from the currency fluctuations on the interest of a foreign bond are much more difficult to understand than the bond itself. Because of this confusion, banks can sell the parts for more than the whole.

CAO CAO TROUBLES THE ENEMY CAMP Cao Cao, the warlord of Wei who fell for *The stratagem of sowing discord*, faced a difficult decision while laying siege to a rival city. His forces had established a position outside an entrenched enemy. His army was strong but was running low on supplies—so low, in fact, that his soldiers would likely starve before completing their mission. Cao Cao had two choices: He could retreat or risk losing to hunger. The logical choice was to retreat. This would at least allow him to succeed another day.

But Cao Cao decided to apply *Trouble the water to catch the fish* with the hope of winning the battle quickly.

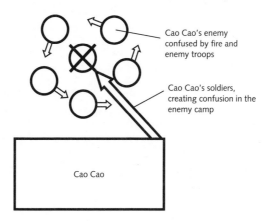

Cao Cao's enemy confused by fire and enemy troops

Cao Cao's soldiers, creating confusion in the enemy camp

Cao Cao

He dressed a group of soldiers in enemy uniforms and had them march toward the enemy camp. At the camp gates his men convinced the guards that they were reinforcements, and entered the enemy camp. Soon after, his men set fire to the enemy's tents and supplies.

As confusion ensued, the enemy's army was torn between dousing the fires and battling the invaders. Complicating the situation, they could not distinguish between their own troops and Cao Cao's, who wore the same armor. Blinded by fire and chaos, the enemy did not see Cao Cao's army encroaching from beyond the stronghold's walls. Cao Cao took the stronghold.

SUMMARY By linking things that are normally separate, or separating things that are normally linked, we can "trouble the water" around our adversaries (consumers, partners, competitors, and so forth). This freezes our adversaries (making them less likely to understand our intentions or to see us coming) and increases our chances of success.

PART TWO

WU WEI:
GO WITH THE GRAIN

無為

Wu Wei, a term coined by Lao Tzu, most closely means "go with the flow." It advocates yielding to nature rather than opposing it—being a flexible blade of grass instead of a rigid oak tree.

In the West, we equate power with going against nature's flow, overcoming odds, or forcing an outcome. As Winston Churchill said,

> Never give in, never, never, never, never, in nothing great or small, large
> or petty, never give in except to convictions of honour and good sense.
> Never yield to force; never yield to the apparently overwhelming might
> of the enemy.[i]

The underlying Western assumption is that the world is rigid and will not change unless we act upon it. Great change requires us to expend great effort. The underlying Taoist assumption, however, is that the world is constantly changing, and that by exerting our efforts wisely we can influence this evolving change with minimal effort. The Taoist view is that when we do not feel tired, we have been efficient in impacting the world. As Lao Tzu wrote in the *Tao Te Ching*,

Stiff and unbending is the principle of death.

Gentle and yielding is the principle of life.

Thus an army without flexibility never wins a battle.

A tree that is unbending is easily broken.

The hard and strong will fall.

The soft and weak will overcome.

A story by Chuang Zhu, Lao Tzu's most famous contemporary, illustrates this principle well. A prince praised his cook for the skill with which he cut meat, because the meat appeared to fall effortlessly off the carcass. The cook explained that when he first began to cut animals he saw them as whole animals. Over many years of practice, however, he learned to see the animal's separate parts. This allowed him to slice easily around the parts rather than struggling to cut through them. Average cooks need to change their knives once a month. Good cooks do so once a year. But because the cook in this story learned how to cut efficiently, he did not have to change his knife in nineteen years.

> *What the ancients called a clever fighter is one who not only wins, but excels in winning with ease.*
>
> —SUN TZU, THE ART OF WAR[ii]

The following cases illustrate the power of Wu Wei in action.

Remove the Firewood from Under the Pot

釜底抽薪

When confronted with a powerful enemy, do not fight them
head-on but try to find their weakest spot to initiate their collapse.
This is the weak overcoming strong.

—FROM *THE 36 STRATAGEMS*

POWERFUL COMPANIES do not attach themselves to one source of control. Understanding the complex interdependence of all things, they broaden their view to reveal unorthodox sources of influence. This is seeking the path of least effort and resistance—Wu Wei.

We like to oversimplify the dynamics of competition. We say competition consists of three players: our company, our competitors, and our consumers (the "3-C" model). Within this framework, we focus on key competencies such as being "customer-centric," or "technology driven."

These simplifications help us direct employees and educate investors, but they also limit us. Companies without such preferences for simplicity have more freedom. They play pieces their competitors never knew were on the game board. While one company decides where to exert power, its opponent, following the stratagem *Remove the firewood from under the pot*, attacks the source of this power.

KEY ELEMENTS:

- Rather than engage your adversary head-on, you attack his source of power

- This weakens your adversary or hinders his ability to attack

- You defeat your weakened adversary

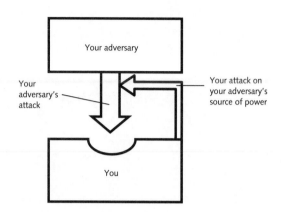

ATTACK THE FUEL When Coca-Cola converted from sugar to high-fructose corn syrup as its main sweetening ingredient, it attempted to "lock up" supply by signing large, long-term supply contracts with corn syrup manufacturers. It did this, of course, to limit Pepsi-Cola's access to the sweetener, thus hindering Pepsi's efforts to introduce its own high-fructose corn syrup–based product.

By the late 1980s, Sony had become a world-leading consumer electronics company. Because it believed that its core products were becoming commodities, it launched a strategy to expand its control further upstream to the content that fed its devices. It purchased Columbia Pictures and CBS with the intention of using their content to fuel the sale of Sony devices and to ensure that these companies would not deny content to Sony.

Perhaps the most well known application of this tactic involves Minnetonka, the maker of Softsoap. The small company realized that if its new Softsoap products were successful, more powerful consumer goods companies like Procter & Gamble and Colgate-Palmolive would quickly introduce their own liquid soap products and leverage their marketing and distribution muscle to overtake Minnetonka. So the company signed large, long-term contracts with the manufacturers of the pumps that were needed to produce liquid soap products. By locking up a large share of the pump supply, Minnetonka hindered P&G's and Colgate-Palmolive's attempts to follow with competing products (because these companies could not get enough pumps). This strategy afforded Minnetonka sufficient time to establish a defensible position. While most small companies that go head-to-head with P&G and Colgate-Palmolive fail, Minnetonka survived.

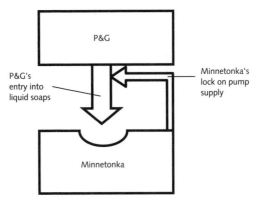

In each of these cases, the attacker targeted its enemy's source of power. This approach allows a more efficient application of power than does the traditional approach of attacking the enemy directly.

HAN STARVES REBELS In 154 B.C., nine states collaborated to stage a rebellion against the ruling Han Empire in China. The Han general calculated that he did not have the power to quell this uprising head-on. So he attacked the rebels' supply lines.

He ordered his primary troops to assemble as if preparing for battle while he led a group of smaller, more lightly armed troops around the battlefield. This smaller group raced behind the amassing rebel forces and set up position on a key route on which the rebels would later depend for supplies.

The Han general then ordered his primary troops to engage the rebel force without launching a genuine attack. The main forces engaged. The rebels were pleased that they were sustaining the "attack" so well when, after some time, they realized their supply lines had been cut. Their sol-

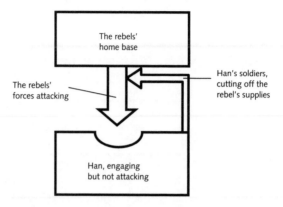

diers grew hungry and thirsty, but no food or water came to recharge them. Forced to fight on, the soldiers lost first their passion, then their energy, and finally their will to rebel. In this way, Han ended the rebellion with little cost or effort.

SUMMARY Attacking your adversary's supply lines requires less effort than directly attacking him. A hungry adversary is easier to take. So cut off your adversary's supply lines, starve him, and only then attack.

> When the soldiers stand leaning on their spears, they are faint from want
> of food. If those who are sent to draw water begin by drinking themselves,
> the army is suffering from thirst.
>
> —SUN TZU, THE ART OF WAR[iii]

Shut the Door to Capture the Thief

關門捉賊

When dealing with a small and weak enemy, surround and destroy him.
If you let him retreat, you will be at a disadvantage in pursuing him.

—FROM *THE 36 STRATAGEMS*

WHEN OUR ADVERSARY is relatively weak, we can seize the moment without necessarily attacking directly. Rather it is both effective and efficient to simply contain him. Surrounding our adversary is effective because it prevents him from launching a counter attack against us somewhere else later. We have in effect neutralized him. It is efficient because it often requires less energy than a direct attack would and yet it offers the same benefit of rendering our adversary unable to cause us harm.

As industries' structures evolve, power shifts from one company to another, from buyers to suppliers, and from companies to customers and back to customers. We should strive to build on each favorable gust of power. Wu Wei implies we should choose the time and method that minimizes effort. This means exerting control over our adversaries when they are weak or divided. And doing so by moving around them, rather than directly at them.

KEY ELEMENTS:

- You encounter a moment when your opponent is weak, divided, or dispersed

You shutting the door

Your weakened adversary

You

- You capitalize on this moment by surrounding your enemy, preventing escape, but avoid direct attack

NINTENDO SHUTS THE DOOR TO SECURE SUCCESS Consider how Nintendo capitalized on its strength early in the video game wars. As a pioneer, and early leader, Nintendo commanded the largest user base of any game console manufacturers. This made Nintendo the software developers' favorite platform. Developers could make much more money writing programs for Nintendo than they could anywhere else.

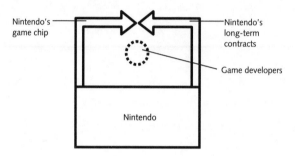

Of course, Nintendo also depended heavily on its game developers. It needed an attractive library of proprietary games to maintain its lead. So the company decided to exert its power over game developers, not by attacking them directly (e.g., by taking them over) but by containing them using two initiatives:

- Nintendo built a security chip into its console to prevent gamers from using software from other systems. As a result, developers could not reach Nintendo consumers by developing for other platforms

- It forced developers to sign exclusivity agreements that prevented them from selling a title to another company for two years after it had been released on Nintendo.

Software developers had two options: (1) they could build software for non-Nintendo consoles with no hope of selling to Nintendo's wide user base or (2) they could write for Nintendo exclusively. Developers consistently, and logically, chose option two.

By shutting the door on developers, because developers had no freedom to sell to others, when Nintendo was the only game in town, Nintendo was able to set up a barrier to entry that extended its competitive lead for years.

QIN SHUTS THE DOOR ON ZHAO In 260 B.C., two great states, Qin and Zhao, met in a decisive battle. By seizing on a moment of weakness, Qin shut the door on—and, as a result, soundly defeated—its enemy.

The armies of Qin and Zhao were locked in an even battle when the Zhao army replaced its experienced commander with a less-experienced but promising new one. The Qin general saw this switch as an opportunity to apply the stratagem *Shut the door to capture the thief.*

He attacked the Zhao army, then feigned a retreat to draw the Zhao troops out. The new Zhao commander pushed his troops in pursuit into Qin territory. But he soon realized his mistake. The Qin army had

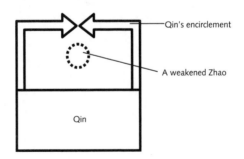

retreated to the sides rather than straight back, and reassembled behind the Zhao forces. The Zhao general and his 40,000 troops were surrounded. The Zhao army tried to retreat, but the Qin had them trapped.

The Qin had their enemy surrounded but they did not close in for the kill. They held their position for over a month during which time the

Zhao army repeatedly tried to break Qin's grasp. Qin never gave in, but never closed in either.

As supplies ran low, the Zhao soldiers grew weak. Without outside communication they grew desperate. Finally, after forty-six days, the Zhao commander gathered his best troops and made a final attempt to break out. He died in the process.

With the Zhao soldiers leaderless, hungry, and desperate, the Qin marched in and slaughtered the remaining Zhao soldiers, thus ending the long rivalry.

> *That the impact of your army may be like a grindstone dashed against an egg—this is effected by the science of weak points and strong.*
> —SUN TZU, *THE ART OF WAR*[iv]

SUMMARY Even when contending with a weaker adversary whom we have the power to defeat, we may be better off letting them survive. By following the course that Nintendo and the Qin each followed to remove their adversary's threat, by containing our adversary instead of attacking him, we can secure safety while preserving our energy.

Replace the Beams with Rotten Timbers

偷樑換柱

Make the allied forces change their battle formation frequently so that their main strength will be taken away. When they collapse by themselves, go and swallow them up. This is like pulling back the wheels of a chariot to control its direction.

—from *The 36 Stratagems*

W u Wei implies we attack where our efforts are most rewarded. By destroying our adversary's support structure we can bring him down completely and efficiently.

The terms "beam" and "pillar" here have literal military meanings. They relate to battle formations. A typical battle formation in Chinese warfare consisted of two axles: A central axle (called the "heavenly beam"), which extended from the front to the rear of a formation, and a horizontal axle (called the "earthly pillar"), which connected the left and right flanks. The best soldiers fought along one of theses axles.

This stratagem advises we manipulate our opponent's axles so that they lose their integrity. Like rotten timbers, they will crumble. In the ensuing chaos we can easily secure victory.

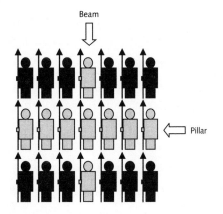

KEY ELEMENTS:

- Your adversary's
  advantage is built
  on key support
  structures

- You attack
  these structures

- By breaking his key
  support structures,
  your adversary's
  integrity falters;
  then you take him

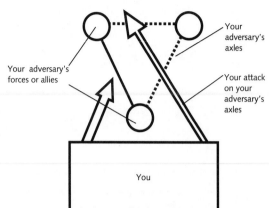

When the general is weak and without authority; when his orders are not clear and distinct; when there are no fixed duties assigned to officers and men, and the ranks are formed in a slovenly haphazard manner, the result is utter disorganization.

—SUN TZU, *THE ART OF WAR*[v]

Our competitor's advantage is constructed like a house. On its surface it appears to be a cohesive whole. But dissection reveals some elements, such as painted sideboards, that are cosmetic; others, such as beams, that provide critical support; and still others, such as the foundation, that are too fundamental to upset. Companies that damage other companies' critical, yet vulnerable supports can decrease their adversary's advantage with minimal effort. This is like destroying a house by knocking down its supporting beams.

COMPETITIVE BEAMS As described before, a key success factor in the video game console business is having a library of popular games. Without this, a machine will not sell.

No game console manufacturer depends as heavily on its game library as Nintendo does. Its roster includes two of the most well known game brands: Mario Brothers and Donkey Kong. Unlike other game consoles, Nintendo relies exclusively on games to sell its machine. Sony and Microsoft market their machines as DVD and CD players as well as game consoles. Nintendo's machines are purely for play.

So if a competitor wanted to bring down Nintendo, it could do so most completely by attacking Nintendo's source of games, as Sony did with PlayStation 2. Nintendo had long used its dominant position to control independent game developers (see *Shut the door to capture the thief*). By requiring exclusivity agreements and forcing game developers to write for a technology that could only be used in Nintendo machines, Nintendo maintained a hold on developers. Sony attacked this hold.

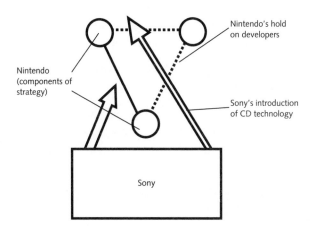

It introduced a CD-based system for which it was easier to create programs and that was less costly and bulky than Nintendo's silicone-cartridge format. In this way Sony made it less risky for game developers to abandon Nintendo. Its tactic worked. Game developers began switching allegiances to Sony in droves.

Nintendo was slow to respond. It held on to its silicone-cartridge format for years. This further alienated game developers and extended the exodus.

Finally, in 2001, Nintendo caved in. It converted to an optical disk technology with its GameCube product. This technology approximated the ease and cost of developing for CDs. But by then Sony had toppled Nintendo's dominance.

JIN TOPPLES QIN In A.D. 383, during the Six Dynasties Period in China, two empires of unequal power—Qin and Jin—faced off in a stalemate. The smaller empire saved itself by manipulating its adversary's beams.

The stronger empire, Qin, was attempting to destroy a much weaker one, Jin. The Qin army was encamped just across a river that bordered Jin territory. Despite Qin's relative strength (Jin was smaller and undergoing internal conflict), there were two reasons why the Qin general did not want to cross the river to attack the enemy. First, some clever maneuvering by Jin had given him the false impression that the Jin army was less vulnerable than it actually was. Second, the army that crosses the river is always at a disadvantage to the one waiting on the shore. For this second reason the Jin army also refused to cross the river, hence the stalemate.

To break the stalemate and free his empire from threat, the Jin general devised a plan to disrupt the Qin army's axles, destroy the integrity of its formations, and force it to retreat.

His first step was to send an envoy to the Qin general with a deceptive proposition: that he pull back his troops to allow the Jin army to cross the river. The two could then fight on solid ground and settle the conflict.

The Qin general conferred with his advisors and decided on the following plan: He would accept Jin's proposal and order his troops to retreat. But once the Jin army was halfway across the river, he would reverse his orders and attack. The Jin army, caught in the river, would fall quickly.

The Jin general expected, even counted on, Qin deceit. He ordered a few of his men to dress as Qin soldiers and infiltrate the Qin camps to spread a rumor: that their general had discovered the Jin army was actually much stronger that he originally believed it to be and that he feared they would lose the battle if the Jin crossed the river.

The next day the Qin general ordered his troops to retreat as promised. The troops did not know that this retreat was prearranged, and they took it as a sign that the rumors were true—that the Jin army really was much stronger and they were at risk of losing their lives. So instead of retreating in an orderly manner, panic broke out. The Qin soldiers abandoned their formations, dropped their weapons, and ran.

The Qin general lost control in the chaos. He ordered his troops to return to battle but, because their formation and command-control structure had fallen apart, the orders disappeared in the wind. His men kept running. His house crumbled because his beams and pillars had been destroyed. Jin was saved.

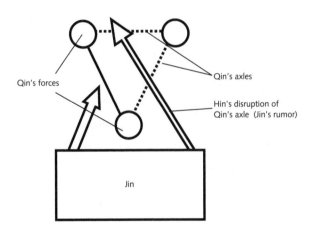

Qin's forces

Qin's axles

Hin's disruption of
Qin's axle (Jin's rumor)

Jin

SUMMARY Jin and Sony each focused their efforts on the support structures on which their adversary most depended. By pulling out these supports, they were able to make their adversaries collapse into themselves.

The Stratagem of the Beautiful Woman

美人計

*When faced with a formidable enemy, try to subdue their leader. When dealing with
an able and resourceful commander, exploit his indulgence of sensual pleasures in
order to weaken his fighting spirit. When the commander becomes inept, his soldiers
will demoralize, and their combat power will be greatly weakened. This stratagem
takes advantage of the enemy's weakness for the sake of self-protection.*

—FROM *THE 36 STRATAGEMS*

THE "BEAUTIFUL WOMAN" HERE symbolizes something our adversary needs or desires. By introducing whatever this thing is, we can
control our adversary's behavior by (1) distracting him or (2) manipulating him. In this way our adversary becomes our puppet.

KEY ELEMENTS:

- Your adversary has a
  weakness or need

- You bait your adver-
  sary by feeding this
  weakness or need

- This encourages
  your adversary to act in
  a way counter to his benefit

- You take advantage of
  his misstep

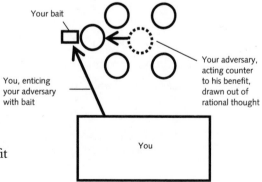

BEAUTIFUL MONEY When Microsoft woke up to the Internet's relevance around 1995, it launched what many considered desperate
attempts to build new Internet businesses. Although the company took
six years in this effort, it cut seemingly insurmountable leads by catching
up to the top portals and ISPs. Microsoft owes some of its success to
pulling a lever that its competitors could not pull.

Microsoft struggled against an uncommon constraint while building its ISP business. For legal and political reasons, it could not rely on
its usual strategy of giving new products a preferable presence on the
Windows operating system. This strategy had enabled Microsoft to
leverage its Windows asset to provide competitive advantage to other
products (see *Besiege Wei to rescue Zhao*). But competitors and the government forced Microsoft to treat its MSN ISP service and competing
ISP services equally.

However, Microsoft found a substitute source of influence. The
retailer that sells a customer a new computer can influence the customer's
choice of access provider. Microsoft decided to exert its power on retailers by offering them something they needed badly at the time—money.

Traditional retailers were struggling against direct-to-consumer chan-
nels (such as Dell) and online retailers for investor attention. Investors
were dropping retailer valuations. Retailers needed investment to buoy
their stocks and to fund initiatives that would maintain their relevance in
what many believed would be an online dominated world.

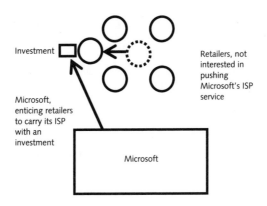

So Microsoft made a series of investments in key computer retailers—it invested $100 million in Radio Shack and $200 million in Best Buy—in exchange for these retailers promoting its Internet service provider.

A WOMAN TOPPLES AN EMPIRE Around 200 B.C. a ruthless warlord, Dong Zhou, indirectly controlled the Han Empire through a puppet emperor. He strengthened his power by adopting a powerful warrior, Lu Bu, as his son, thereby ensuring Lu Bu's and the army's loyalty. With this solid power base Dong Zhou was able to rule with a heavy hand and with little fear of recourse. He developed a reputation for regularly beheading those who betrayed, contradicted, or opposed him.

The governor of one of the empire's provinces feared it was only a matter of time before he, too, was ordered killed, so he devised a plan to remove Dong Zhou from power. He applied *The stratagem of the beautiful woman.*

The governor first found a stunning young woman who was willing to help him execute his plan. He then invited the warrior Lu Bu to his house for dinner and had the young woman serve Lu Bu wine. The young woman quickly intrigued Lu Bu. His curiosity grew as he drank, and eventually he asked the governor about the young woman. The governor said she was his niece and offered her to Lu Bu as his wife. Lu Bu eagerly accepted and made arrangements for a wedding. The governor's first stone was in place.

Next, the governor invited the warlord Dong Zhou over for dinner. And again, in a similar fashion, the governor conspicuously displayed the young woman so that Dong Zhou became enamored and inquired after her. The governor told the warlord she was his maid and offered her to the warlord as his concubine. The warlord enthusiastically accepted and arranged for his people to pick her up the next day. The governor's second stone was in place.

Through the woman, the governor gained influence over the two most powerful people in the empire. The governor used this influence to

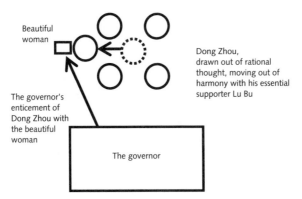

Beautiful woman

Dong Zhou, drawn out of rational thought, moving out of harmony with his essential supporter Lu Bu

The governor's enticement of Dong Zhou with the beautiful woman

The governor

play Dong Zhou and Lu Bu against each other. Each thought the other was trying to steal the woman against her will. The woman lied to each to reinforce this belief, asking the warlord to protect her from the warrior and vice versa.

The rivalry between the warlord and his chief warrior heated up. Neither was willing to give in. Lu Bu eventually killed Don Zhou and so freed the governor and the Han Empire from Dong Zhou's oppressive rule.

SUMMARY We can use that which our adversary wants or needs to induce him to follow our wishes. The governor dangled a woman on his hook and Microsoft dangled money.

This tactic may at first seem elementary, but this is because we often and unnecessarily limit its scope. We tend to consider only levers of influence consistent with our environment. For example, if we want to influence a supplier, we concentrate on levers that fall within the scope of a buyer-supplier relationship (e.g., payment terms and logistics); if we want to influence a distributor, we consider margins and marketing support.

Companies that think beyond the limits set by context and consider a broad array of options can exert greater power more efficiently. They uncover unorthodox sources of leverage for which their adversaries are unprepared.

Beat the Grass to Startle the Snake

打草驚蛇

Any suspicion about the enemy's circumstances must be investigated.
Before any military action, be sure to ascertain the enemy's situation; repeated
reconnaissance is an effective way to discover the hidden enemy.

—FROM *THE 36 STRATAGEMS*

I N THE CONTEXT of *The 36 Stratagems*, Microsoft's persistent trial-and-error approach is best referred to as *Beat the grass to startle the snake*. This tactic suggests that rather than committing to a full attack, we should make a series of smaller attacks in order to learn our adversary's strengths and likely responses. With this knowledge we can defeat our adversary more easily.

KEY ELEMENTS:

- You are unsure of your enemy's strength or strategy

- You launch a small-scale or indirect attack on your adversary

- Your adversary reveals his strength or strategy by his response to your "false" attack

- You plan your "real" attack with this new knowledge

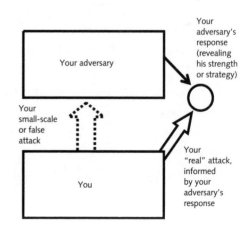

When you approach a bush in which you fear a poisonous snake hides, you can beat the bush with a stick. If a snake is hiding, it will either strike or run away. Either way, you will know if the bush is safe, and can decide where to place your next step with this information.

Miyamoto Musashi, a famous Japanese sword master and author of *The Book of Five Rings*, calls this tactic "Moving Shadows":

> Moving shadows is something you do when you cannot discern what an adversary is thinking.
>
> In large-scale military science, when you cannot discern the enemy state, you pretend to make a powerful attack to see what they will do. Having seen the opponent's methods, it is easy to seize victory by taking advantage of the different tactics specially adapted to each use.
>
> —MIYAMOTO MUSASHI, *THE BOOK OF FIVE RINGS*[vi]

This stratagem delivers power by inducing an adversary to react, thereby extracting information about the adversary's strength or intentions. Action is pregnant with information. A story of two master swordsmen illustrates this well.

Two swordsmen, both old and experienced, stood opposite each other prepared to spar in competition. The referee announced that the match should begin, but neither swordsman moved. They stood still for several minutes until the referee called the match a draw. Neither moved because action would reveal information (e.g., how the opponent's weight was distributed, the direction of his momentum) that his opponent could use against him. If we force our opponent to react without committing ourselves, we gain an advantage.

PERSIST Microsoft's approach to establishing MSN is indicative of an effective tactic: crafting a strategy of small, indirect attacks rather than large, decisive ones. This approach is quite common to Microsoft and other highly competitive companies. Most Westerners perceive the success of highly competitive companies to be built on exhaustive strategizing and committed execution. Yet this is rarely the case. In accordance with Wu Wei, successful companies usually take a series of small, incremental steps that preserve energy, minimize risk, and allow them to "feel out" the market.

Microsoft's history is filled with the same pattern of trial and error. It is not that Microsoft identifies opportunities before its competition; indeed, Microsoft is often a follower. The image of Microsoft thrusting into new territory and cutting down the competition through blitzkrieg warfare is, for the most part, inaccurate. Microsoft follows a patient, deliberate approach that allows it to feel out the competition as it works its way into a leading position over the course of many years.

Microsoft's entry into the Web is an interesting example. When the company introduced its portal in the mid 1990s, industry experts believed it had missed its opportunity to be an Internet player because Yahoo! and AOL had already built insurmountable leads. The often-cited fact was that Bill Gates did not mention the Internet in the first version of his 1995 book *The Road Ahead*, so the publisher rapidly produced a revised version that did. But Microsoft persisted, buoyed by strong cash reserves and minimal debt.

In comparison to Yahoo!'s and AOL's breakneck rises to power, MSN's six-year-long effort seems like a slow plod. Its execution was plagued with mistakes—and with each of these mistakes, onlookers cheered for the smaller, independent companies like Yahoo! and AOL who taught the software giant lessons about the Internet and the new economy. And therein lies a key to Microsoft's success. Most observers interpreted Microsoft's failures as faults. But these missteps also offered lessons. With each loss, Microsoft learned about its market and its competitors. It then informed its next attack with this new knowledge. Through a sequence of minor battles, Microsoft learned. With each loss, it grew more familiar with competitive and consumer dynamics to cut further into its competitors' leads. After six years MSN became one of the top Web destinations.

Its server software business followed a similar pattern. When Microsoft first entered the segment, industry experts discounted, even poked fun at, the company's prospects. But Microsoft persisted for a decade to slowly build a legitimate position. Today it commands nearly 50 percent of the market.

> *Float a trial balloon to see how well something is accepted and received, especially when you doubt its popularity or success.*
>
> —Baltasar Gracian, *The Art of Worldly Wisdom*[vii]

BEAT AN ASSISTANT TO STARTLE A MAGISTRATE Although this stratagem is much older, its modern name originates from a story during the Tang dynasty (618–907). The story centers around a provincial magistrate who regularly accepted bribes. His citizens, who had gotten fed up

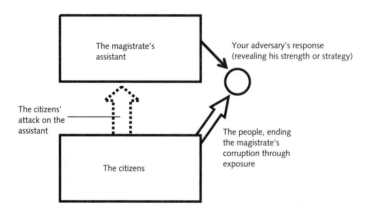

with the corruption, issued a formal complaint. But rather than issue a complaint directly implicating the magistrate, they issued charges against one of his assistant magistrates. Perhaps the citizens feared the response that a direct attack on the magistrate might evoke. Perhaps they were not sure whether the magistrate was actually involved. Either way, their tactic had the desired effect: They startled and exposed the snake.

The magistrate felt the threat and ended his corrupt practices. In a moment of anxiety, the magistrate wrote: "You merely beat the grass, but by doing so startle the snake within."

SUMMARY By staging a small, uncommitted attack, we can learn how our adversaries and markets will react to a real attack. Our subsequent attacks then become better informed and, thus, more effective.

Loot a Burning House

趁火打劫

When the enemy falls into severe crisis, exploit his adversity and attack
by direct confrontation. This is the strong defeating the weak.

—FROM *THE 36 STRATAGEMS*

B USINESSES THAT CONSISTENTLY seize on others' misfortunes build power. They act like water, exerting pressure on all surfaces, so that the moment an opening appears they are already advancing. A key element of this approach is to see opportunity where others see trouble. Birds fear floods. But the bird that can become a fish will thrive where other birds perish. Such flexibility is in accordance with Wu Wei. Coca-Cola and Kiwi Airlines both adopt aggressive, fluid opportunity-chasing strategies, exemplifying the stratagem *Loot a burning house.*

KEY ELEMENTS:

- Trouble strikes
- Your adversary freezes or retreats
- You capitalize on your adversary's inaction or retreat to build power

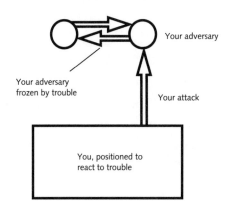

Your adversary

Your adversary
frozen by trouble

Your attack

You, positioned to
react to trouble

When the [enemy] is in chaos, take him.

—SUN TZU, *THE ART OF WAR*[viii]

COCA-COLA ADVANCES INTO BURNING ECONOMIES Coca-Cola owes much of its success to seizing on opportunity where its peers fled trouble. It maintains a state of readiness to capitalize on global, or macroeconomic, trouble.

When the Brazilian economy began to show signs of weakness and the real (the Brazilian currency) devalued by 40 percent in early 1999, foreign companies scrambled to develop plans to pull out of Brazil. Coca-Cola, however, read the situation differently. It saw an opportunity to increase its Brazilian investments at a 40-percent discount and bolster its standing in the country. It quickly announced it would increase investment in the country by 10 percent in that year.

Reacting to new opportunities takes time. Acquisitions and large investments can take months to negotiate. But companies can position themselves to act rapidly by negotiating deals before opportunities strike. Before economic problems hit Eastern Europe in the late 1990s, Coca-Cola had offered $187 million for a bottler owned by Britain's Inchape PLC. The offer was rejected. But when economic problems surfaced, Coca-Cola was poised to act. It bought the bottler for $87 million, less than half its original bid!

In another example of Coca-Cola's readiness creating an advantage, the company outpaced its competitors in reacting to the Mexican peso crisis in 1994. By investing in new plants more quickly than did its competition, Coca-Cola built the capacity to expand its market share in Mexico from 53 percent to 68 percent.

Each gust of opportunity lengthens Coca-Cola's lead because it positions itself to act and because where others see trouble Coca-Cola sees opportunity.

KIWI LOOTS AMERICAN'S BURNING HOUSE American Airlines

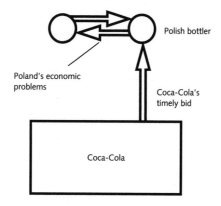

employees went on strike during the Thanksgiving holiday in 1993, leaving thousands of passengers scrambling for alternate flights. Most airlines chose to focus on stealing American Airlines' Thanksgiving business. But Kiwi, a small discount airline, was particularly creative at this strategic moment and benefited disproportionately as a result.

Kiwi specifically targeted American Airlines customers. First, it sent faxes to travel agents advertising availability on Kiwi flights that could substitute for the American flights affected by the strike. It also instructed its agents to give American's customers tailored service, including a "Welcome American Airlines passengers" sign at its ticket counters.

Convincing customers to try a new company is expensive. The American strike created a temporary opportunity for Kiwi to skirt that cost. By reacting quickly, resourcefully, and expediently, Kiwi was able to loot American's customers at bargain basement rates.

YUE CROUCHES FOR FIFTEEN YEARS In the fifth century B.C. the states of Yue and Wu were at war. In a decisive battle in 498 B.C., the Wu army took the emperor of Yue prisoner and forced him into slavery.

For the next three years the emperor of Yue groomed horses for the emperor of Wu. He worked without protest. Indeed, he behaved so respectfully and obediently that he won the Wu emperor's trust. Eventually the Yue emperor gained his freedom and returned to his home.

Although the emperor of Yue yearned for revenge, he waited. In the years that followed his release, he continued to act respectfully toward

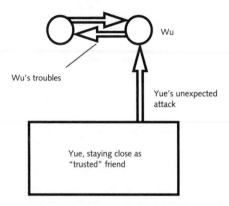

Wu and purposefully stayed close to Wu's emperor. He regularly sent gifts of gold and money to strengthen the foundation of trust between the two nations.

During this time, the Yue emperor rebuilt his army. This took several years. Once this task was complete, more than five years later, he had the strength to attack Wu and exact his revenge.

But he did not. He sent gifts, maintained his friendly countenance, and waited.

Ten years after the Yue emperor's release, a drought hit Wu, and the Yue emperor sensed his moment approaching. When the emperor of Wu foolishly executed his most capable advisor, the Yue emperor prepared to strike. And in 482 B.C., when the emperor of Wu led his most capable troops out of the capital to meet with rulers from surrounding states, the Yue emperor finally seized the moment and unleashed his revenge. He attacked and took the Wu capital.

The Yue emperor sat poised for thirteen years, waiting patiently for a sign of fire. When Wu's house started to burn, he advanced. His timing gave him a clean victory and a satisfying revenge.

So in war, the way is to avoid what is strong and to strike at what is weak. Water shapes its course according to the nature of the ground over which it flows; the soldier works out his victory in relation to the foe whom he is facing. Therefore, just as water retains no constant shape, so in warfare there are no constant conditions.

—SUN TZU, *THE ART OF WAR*[ix]

SUMMARY This stratagem advises that we capitalize on trouble. Trouble creates potential opportunity for two reasons. If it disproportionately weakens our adversary, we gain relative strength, which we can use to gain ground. If the trouble weakens both our adversary and ourselves equally, we can benefit by advancing if, in the face of this trouble, our adversary freezes or retreats.

Sometimes Running Away
Is the Best Strategy

走爲上計

*To avoid combat with a powerful enemy, the whole army
should retreat and wait for the right time to advance again. This is
not inconsistent with normal military principles.*

—FROM *THE 36 STRATAGEMS*

WE HAVE THREE OPTIONS when facing an adversary we cannot defeat. We can surrender, we can make peace, or we can retreat. If we surrender or make peace, we limit future options. But if we retreat, we preserve our strength and maintain the possibility of exerting our power either at a later time or in a different place. Chinese military history is filled with stories of armies that came back from retreat, often after tens of years, to claim ultimate victory.

KEY ELEMENTS:

- You face a powerful
  adversary

- You retreat

- You exert your preserved
  power somewhere else
  or at some other time

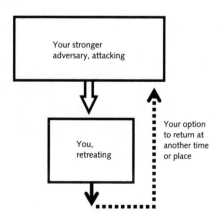

KNOWING WHEN TO EXIT In 1980, when Jack Welch became CEO of General Electric, the company was a reliable but average American conglomerate. Jack wanted to change this, so he gave the first challenge: GE would be number 1 or number 2 in each of its businesses, or it would exit that business.

This strategy met resistance. Some argued that companies that are not number 1 or number 2 can nevertheless be profitable and, with enough time, can become number 1 or number 2. Others argued that Welch feared competition. Welch responded,

> Some people say I'm afraid to compete. I think one of the jobs of a businessperson is to get away from slugfests and into niches where you can prevail. The fundamental goal is to get rid of weaknesses, to find a sheltered womb where no one can hurt you. There's no virtue in looking for a fight. If you're in a fight, your job is to win. But if you can't win, you've got to find a way out.[x]

In other words, it is better to retreat than to surrender or lose. Sometimes running away is the best stratagem.

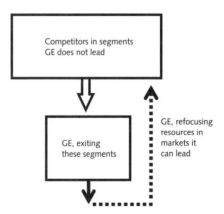

In 1982 GE aggressively divested businesses according to Welch's "number 1 or number 2" strategy, the sales of which generated $8.5 billion in cash. GE then used this cash to expand its efforts in businesses where it could win. This housecleaning laid the foundation for GE's impressive performance over the next twenty years.

By applying the stratagem of "running away," Welch transformed GE. He could have followed the more common strategy of persisting as long as a business is profitable. Indeed, we can argue from a purely mathematical perspective that such a strategy is superior. For various reasons both logical and illogical (e.g., we associate "running away" with failure), we tend to hold on longer than we should. Yet most successful companies show that running away can be a powerful first move. It enables us to invest our resources in more attractive efforts.

SURRENDERING TO RETURN In 1403, during the Ming dynasty, the Ming emperor was considering suicide. His stronghold had been surrounded by an enemy force and was about to fall. But one of his eunuchs stopped him. The eunuch explained that he had instructions from the emperor's grandfather to direct any emperor who faced an apparently hopeless situation to open a particular chest.

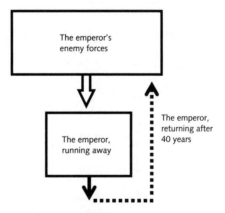

The emperor agreed. He looked in the chest his grandfather had prepared and found a monk's robe, a razor, a diploma, and some silver. His grandfather's message was clear. He escaped through a hidden passage to a monastery, put on the robe, and shaved his head. Disguised as monk, the emperor fled the city as it burned down.

After the siege, the people assumed the emperor had died in the fire. But he had retreated to a remote monastery in the mountains where he lived in obscurity. For the next forty years the emperor practiced the rituals and discipline of a monk.

A rumor began that the old emperor was actually still alive. To address this rumor, the new emperor launched an official inquiry. The inquiry concluded that the rumor was true. The reigning emperor found the old emperor and invited him back into the city, where he was treated with honor. The old emperor lived out the rest of his life in comfort and died a palace guest. He owed this comfortable ending to having run away.

SUMMARY The most clever and powerful are willing to retreat. They do not equate retreat with failure. This is as true for corporations as it is for nations. Though driven to surmount odds, powerful companies recognize when to yield and choose the battles that most reward effort. This requires transcending our attraction to overcoming odds (a tendency strengthened by past successes). It requires that we recognize retreat as an offensive option, one that has benefited armies and politicians for millennia.

Seize the Opportunity to Lead the Sheep Away

順手牽羊

Exploit any minor lapses on the enemy side, and seize every advantage to your side.
Any negligence of the enemy must be turned into a benefit for you.

—FROM *THE 36 STRATAGEMS*

THE NAME OF THIS STRATAGEM originates from a Chinese folk tale about a destitute traveler who, while walking along a country road, comes across a flock of sheep. As he makes his way through it, he notices that the shepherd is preoccupied. So he seizes the opportunity. He emerges from the flock with a sheep in his hands and walks away so calmly and naturally that by the time the shepherd notices the theft, the traveler is gone.

Taking advantage of our opponents' mistakes is in harmony with seeking the path of least effort (Wu Wei). Similar to the stratagem *Loot a burning house*, which advises seizing each opportunity that trouble may offer, the stratagem *Seize the opportunity to lead the sheep away* demonstrates that companies can expand their power by punishing their competitors for each mistake they make.

> *The good fighters of old, first put themselves beyond the possibility of defeat, and then waited for an opportunity of defeating the enemy.*
>
> *To secure ourselves against defeat lies in our own hands, but the opportunity of defeating the enemy is provided by the enemy himself.*
>
> —SUN TZU, *THE ART OF WAR*[xi]

KEY ELEMENTS:

- Your adversary fails to act (e.g., because he is distracted)

- You take advantage of this "deer in the headlights" moment to advance

- By the time your adversary realizes his mistake, you have already taken the advantage

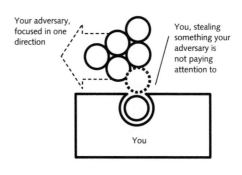

Your adversary, focused in one direction

You, stealing something your adversary is not paying attention to

You

SONY MOVES IN AS OTHERS PAUSE Sony built its leadership in electronics with such a move. In just seven years, Sony transformed itself from being a manufacturer of rice cookers for the Japanese market, to the world leader in the production of consumer radios. It achieved this by seizing on a unique moment when its competitors could not or would not take advantage of a particular opportunity.

When Bell Laboratories invented the transistor in 1947, the two leading electrical and electronics leaders, RCA and GE, agreed with most

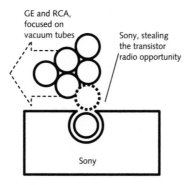

GE and RCA, focused on vacuum tubes

Sony, stealing the transistor radio opportunity

Sony

industry observers that the transistor would one day replace the vacuum tube. But neither RCA nor GE wanted to adopt transistors quickly. Both companies were heavily invested in products designed for vacuum tubes and felt little competitive pressure. So they hesitated. They made plans to study and further develop transistor technology with the goal of replacing vacuum tubes sometime in the next twenty years.

Akio Morita, the CEO of Sony, recognized RCA's and GE's mistake and took advantage of the opening they provided. In the early 1950s he bought a license to use the transistor from Bell Labs for just $25,000. He then challenged his engineers to design a transistor radio faster than the industry believed it could be done. In just two years, far fewer than the twenty RCA and GE had anticipated, Sony introduced a portable transistor radio. For one-third of the cost of a traditional radio, Sony offered consumers a product that was a fraction of a traditional radio's size and weight. Sony went on to dominate the world's consumer radio markets.

This tactic is what Peter Drucker calls "Entrepreneurial Judo." Small attackers can topple large incumbents because the incumbents are too heavily invested in the old way of doing things to embrace a new way.

Sony is not alone in benefiting from this tactic. Home Depot, for example, stole market share from unsuspecting home contractors by convincing consumers to "do it yourself." Contractors could not respond in part because they refused to see Home Depot as a competitor. Coca-Cola's now-famous strategy of attacking water consumers targeted competitors who never had cola on their competitive radar screens. Water companies never saw Coca-Cola as a threat.

Microsoft's seemingly well-calculated strategies tend to depend heavily on this stratagem, as Microsoft's chairman, Bill Gates, admits:

> Most *of our success comes when we end up with a competitor who doesn't do things correctly—that's lucky. You're not supposed to work on a strategy that depends on other people's mistakes, but they've certainly made a lot.*[xii]

SEIZING THE OPPORTUNITY TO TAKE AN "ALLY" In 770 B.C., the state of Song was under siege by an alliance of opposing states. The state of Chen led this alliance. In defense, Song implemented the stratagem of

Beseige Wei to rescue Zhao. It attacked Chen's capital, forcing Chen's aggressors to call off their siege and leave to defend their homes. Through cunning application of this stratagem, Song freed itself from threat.

On its return home the Song army passed through a small state called Tai. Tai had refused to support Song's defense, so Song decided to take the Tai capital in revenge. The Song army surrounded Tai's stronghold and prepared for what promised to be almost certain victory over the weaker Tai state. As it turned out, however, neither state would be victorious.

Tai, facing certain defeat, sent an appeal to Chen for help. When a few days later the Chen army was seen approaching, the Song army called off its siege and hurried home. The Tai army rejoiced. The presence of Chen's powerful army had saved them. The Tai king opened his city gates to welcome the Chen duke and his army.

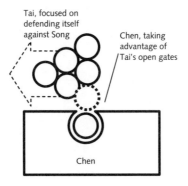

The Chen duke faced an unexpected opportunity. He stood with his army in front of the open city gates of a strategically important state. (Tai was in proximity to Song.) Knowing that an attack on Tai would provoke little or no resistance, he marched his soldiers into the welcoming walls of the Tai capital, kidnapped the Tai king, and took over the city.

Just as the traveler in the Chinese folktale took advantage of an inattentive shepherd, and Sony of an inactive RCA, Tai took advantage of an adversary that it knew could not defend itself. This is the essence of the stratagem. When your adversary is unlikely to react, seize power.

SUMMARY Our adversary will make mistakes, whether for structural reasons (e.g., RCA's decision not to purse development of the transistor aggressively) or because of oversight. By being poised to capitalize on these mistakes, we can consistently gain ground each time our competitor slips.

Feign Madness But Keep Your Balance

假痴不癲

*At times, it is better to pretend to be foolish and do nothing than to brag
about yourself and act recklessly. Be composed and plot secretly, like thunder clouds
hiding themselves during winter only to bolt out when the time is right.*

—FROM *THE 36 STRATAGEMS*

CONCENTRATED FORCE generates an opposing force. A key to achieving our objectives with minimal effort is to avoid triggering this opposing force. Companies that can deliver a threat without it appearing as such can penetrate their competition more easily. Virgin, for example, cultivates an image of irrational irreverence that helps facilitate its entry into new markets.

KEY ELEMENTS:

- Your adversary is powerful and/or you are weak

- You appear mad or incapable in order to avoid being perceived as a threat

- When your adversary puts down his guard, you take him

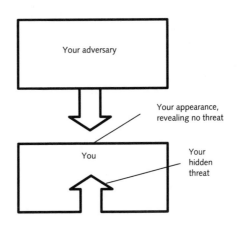

Never let them know what you're thinking.

—MICHAEL CORLEONE, IN *THE GODFATHER* BY MARIO PUZO

VIRGIN'S CRAZY TELEPHONE CALL TO BOEING In 1984, when the Virgin Group announced plans to enter the airline business, most people wrote off the idea. Many airlines had tried to compete with British Airways in the past, but none had had the financing to persevere against the powerful national airline.

Most companies would fight such pessimism with arguments grounded in rational analysis and strategic logic. However, Richard Branson, the head of Virgin, appeared to do exactly the opposite. He cultivated a seemingly amateurish story about how he came up with his idea to compete in the airline business: A business acquaintance happened to give him a proposal for a new airline. Branson called People's Express (British Airways' competition) over the weekend and was encouraged to find they never answered the phone. This pointed to an opportunity in

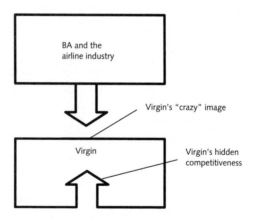

his mind. On Monday he cold-called Boeing to enquire about leasing a used plane. With that he "had done all the market research [he] felt [he] needed and had made up [his] mind."[xiii]

Virgin further bolstered an offbeat image with a series of outlandish publicity events. For example, for Virgin Atlantic's maiden transatlantic flight, Branson dressed up as pirate and filled the plane with champagne and music stars.

These tactics benefited Virgin in more ways than one. They helped build awareness and endearment among fliers. But they also helped keep British Airways off guard. It was unclear, for example, how seriously the national airline should take Virgin. Would Virgin's "crazy" image, which contrasted starkly with British Airways' buttoned-up reputation, make Virgin more or less threatening than other start-ups of the past? British Airways ultimately took Virgin's threat seriously and fought back vigorously, using all the strength it had. It is difficult to know for sure, but many believe that Virgin's unorthodox approach created a gap or softening in British Airways' response, within which Virgin built momentum. As the *Economist* stated in an article outlining the folly of Virgin's entry into the rail business, "To be fair, back in 1984 Mr Branson's entry into the airline business also seemed both a crazy gamble and a threat to his brand."[xiv]

MADNESS CREATES OPPORTUNITY In A.D. 249, General Cao Shuang, who had invested ten years securing near-complete control over his state, lost his power in just four days when he turned his back on a seemingly weak adversary.

Cao Shuang, and his adversary, Sima Yi, were officials of the Wei empire. When the emperor of Wei died and enthroned his young son to

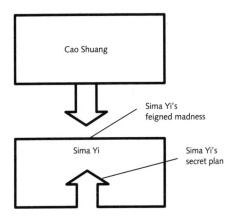

replace him, both Cao Shuang and Sima Yi were charged with looking after the young prince until he reached sufficient age to rule.

Although they initially enjoyed equal power, Cao Shuang ultimately took power from Sima Yi by demanding complete control over the military. Marginalized, Sima Yi feared that Cao Shuang would soon kill him. So he acted crazy. When one of Cao Shuang's henchmen came to visit Sima Yi, Sima Yi acted sick and senile. He spilled soup on his collar to appear weak. He pretended to misunderstand their conversation, to appear senile.

Cao Shuang concluded that Sima Yi posed no threat. He let Sima Yi live and eventually slip from his mind. No longer under heavy scrutiny, Sima Yi waited patiently for an opening. His opportunity came when Cao Shuang left the capital with the young emperor to visit the imperial tombs. Sima Yi quickly gathered his sons and followers and staged a coup. Four days later Sima Yi took control of Wei and had Cao Shuang executed.

By feigning madness we can bide our time in relative anonymity and wait for the right moment to act.

Make use of folly. Even the wisest person sometimes puts this piece into play, and there are occasions when the greatest knowledge lies in appearing to have none.

—BALTASAR GRACIAN, *THE ART OF WORLDLY WISDOM*[xv]

SUMMARY To preempt opposition, avoid appearing a threat. When we appear "crazy" instead of calculating, our adversary will discount our efforts and give us room to succeed.

PART THREE

Wu Chang:
Continuous Change

無常

OUR MENTAL MODEL for what "change" should be and how it affects us has a powerful impact on our actions. It invisibly guides our thinking telling us what type of "change" our action will cause, and whether and when we can take such action. While our mental model may help us to decide which actions to take, it also limits our options and freedom by telling us which action we should not take. For many of us, it is difficult to see our mental models at work because they have been with us nearly our entire lives and so are familiar to the point of appearing to be the truth. We have been so submerged in our mental models of change that we can no longer see them—just as a fish can no longer see the ocean. This is not to say that one's familiar model for change is inaccurate or wrong. The point is using the same model over and over again contributes to our rigidity and makes us predictable, thereby reducing our competitiveness.

By dissecting our mental models for change, and even adopting alternative models, we become more competitive. Companies that regularly outmaneuver their adversaries have a reputation for thinking "out of the box," acting in ways that are inconsistent with the dictates of old predictable models. By adopting alternative concepts of change, we too can become out-of-the-box thinkers, more competitive adversaries, and more skilled at capturing power. Our first step to freeing ourselves from our old model for change—for becoming more creative, out-of-the-box strategists—is to dissect our familiar model, which rests on two key assumptions:

- That the past determines the present (or cause and effect drive change)
- That change connects static moments

THE WESTERN VIEW The West's first key assumption about change is that the past determines the present. Change, in our understanding, is rooted in cause and effect: A cause in the past affects a change in the present. We envision the universe as a game of pool where a linear chain of interactions—one ball knocks against another, propelling it into yet another—explains why any particular ball rests where it does. We can work backward to understand how a particular ball came to stand where it stands and forward to predict what balls we must set in motion to cause our desired result (e.g., 8 ball in the side pocket).

Our second key assumption is that change connects static moments. This means that we divide our lives into two distinct states: rest and motion, or static and kinetic, or no change and change. We call "change" that which happens *between* states of rest. In fact, *Webster's New Universal Unabridged Dictionary* defines "change" as *the passing from one place, state, form, or phase to another.*

We don't question this model, because it seems to work for us and helps us to manage our lives. We believe that it is easier to play games when the balls are at rest than in motion. In the West, life is like a game of pool, ruled by linear sequences of cause and effect, composed of distinct states of change and static moments. This model is not wrong or more limiting than other models but is only limiting if it is the only model we choose.

We would be better off being able to look at our problems through additional lenses.

THE EASTERN VIEW The Eastern view, primarily the Taoist perspective of change, offers an intriguing alternative. Instead of viewing life as composed of static and fluid moments, a Taoist views all moments as change, where the balls never come to rest. This means that instead of looking to the past to understand the present, we just look to the present.

A Taoist takes an entirely different approach to understanding the present, believing that we should look at the present—at that which is occurring—rather than at the past. This does not mean we should not learn from the past, but that the lessons from the past do not hold predictive value. They may help us to recognize patterns (when A happens, B also happens) that in turn help us understand the present and future (A is happening, so B must also be happening). We can see these patterns in all aspects of life, from the flow of a stream around a rock, to the migration of animals through the mountains, to the rise of a new religion around a rigid government. As Westerners, we might be tempted to explain such a pattern through causal relationships. A Taoist view, on the other hand, puts little value in this exercise. Explaining patterns through causal relationships does not necessarily reflect the way the universe works, nor does it improve our attempts to influence or predict our environment. Instead, we should simply learn to recognize life's patterns, and look for them in the current moment.

The Eastern point of view is linked to an interesting understanding of the mechanics of change. While in the West, we view time as a linear sequence of static moments separated by change, the Taoist understanding is cyclical and continuous. Time is a wave in constant motion (*Wu Chang* roughly translates into "nothing is constant"). Points on this wave are always either rising or falling. When the traditional Western view says we are at the top of this wave, the Taoist view says we are already falling.

When the Western view says we are at the bottom, the Taoist view says we are rising. The following Chinese folk story illustrates this view well:

> The horse of a poor farmer ran away. His neighbors visited to offer their condolences, but the farmer said, "Do not feel bad, this may be good fortune." After several weeks, the horse returned to the farmer with another horse of excellent breeding. The farmer's neighbors again visited, this time to congratulate him. But the farmer said, "How do you know this will not lead to disaster?" The farmer bred the horses and became rich. His son liked to ride the horses but one day fell from a horse and broke his leg. When the neighbors came to console him, the father again said, "Do not feel bad, this may be good fortune." A year later barbarians raided the farmer's town and conscripted all young men who could fight. Ninety percent of the young conscripts died in the war, but the farmer's son was left alone because of his bad leg. He lived on.[i]

Most of us cling to static moments. Our victories and failures give us the comfort of feeling like we have just completed a period of change, and we can mark our progress. But for those who embrace change as continuous—unbound by wins, losses, new years, and birthdays—a new definition of "winning" emerges and new options appear. A "game" becomes an endless stream of conflicts rather than a closed-ended event. Winning comes to mean defeating our opponent as often as possible over this endless stream of conflict, not to defeat him or her just once.

In the Taoist view, no loss is permanent. No win is permanent. So exchanging a loss today for future wins becomes more palatable. Indeed, losing is simply an entry to future wins. This is the reason why companies that outthink their competitors often appear to take losing positions only to reemerge as the winner later on. As this chapter illustrates, highly successful companies such as Asahi, Intel, Matsushita, Microsoft, and Sony make decisions that initially appear flawed but that later prove that these companies were already playing the next game while their competitors and the pundits were focusing on the current game.

The Taoist perspective encourages corporations to take longer perspectives. Predicting the future in a linear world driven by causality is difficult, since our accuracy drops off quickly with each cause-and-effect calculation. On the other hand, making long-term predictions in a cyclical world where patterns repeat and moments return is reasonable. Nothing changes permanently, so while we may get some of the details wrong, we are able to predict the overruling pattern quite well.

This was clearly the case with Matsushita. In the early 1930s, Konosuke Matsushita, the founder of the Japanese electrical giant Matsushita, developed ten consecutive 25-year plans that comprised a 250-year corporate strategy. For Western companies using a linear causal model to predict the future, such an exercise would be inaccurate to the point of uselessness. For them, a ten-year planning period is already aggressive.

	WESTERN	TAOIST
Present events are determined by:	Past events	Other present events
Time is:	Linear	Cyclical
Change occurs:	Between events	Continuously
A reasonable planning time frame is:	Up to 10 years	Up to 100+ years
Objective:	Win this war	Win as many wars as possible

In summary, adapting a Taoist perspective, whereby change is continuous and unending, may feel unnatural. However, the process can enable us to better outwit our competition—not because this perspective is right, but because it is different and therefore expands our creativity.

Companies that adopt this perspective are more comfortable peering further out into the future. They often give the impression of making losing decisions today that turn out to be winning decisions over the long-term. As a result, they think one step beyond their competition. And they are already preparing for the next game that will begin when their competition finally catches up to them.

Watch the Fire on the Other Shore

隔岸觀火

When a serious conflict breaks out within the enemy alliance,
wait quietly for the chaos to build. Because once its internal conflict intensifies,
the alliance will bring destruction upon itself. As for you, observe closely and
make preparations for any advantage that may come from it.

—FROM *THE 36 STRATAGEMS*

A LINEAR VIEW OF CHANGE pressures us to take action even when inaction is the best choice. This linear and Western view warns us that our ship will sail out of sight if we pass up the opportunity to act immediately. A cyclical view, however, argues that the wind will shift, the rudder will turn, and our ship will return to us.

Companies that are driven to expand their power, and yet are willing to be patient, will be more competitive in the long run. *The 36 Stratagems* calls this tactic of inaction *Watch the fire on the other shore.*

KEY ELEMENTS:

- Your adversary is engaged in internal conflict or in conflict with other allies

- Your attack might unify your adversary (and her allies)

- You refrain from acting

Your adversary, engaged
in (internal) conflict

You, observing,
refraining from action

- Allowed to continue, the internal conflict damages your adversary
- After your adversary is adequately weakened, you attack

Inaction can be more powerful than action. If aggression drives us to act when we should not, we not only lose power—we also lose opportunity.

THE COST OF ACTION Stories of companies that acted when they should have held back litter business history. One of the most well-known stories is that of Epson's entry into the laser printer business. Epson dominated the low-end dot matrix business, offering customers lower resolution at prices lower than the newer laser printers. But in the early 1990s, Epson decided to expand into laser printers; it was attracted by the higher prices. Epson introduced a laser printer at a discount 5 percent below comparable products.

This move triggered a price war that cut laser printer prices considerably. Indeed, prices fell to a level where laser printers became attractive substitutes for dot matrix printers. Customers then abandoned Epson's dot matrix printers for laser printers, which more often were made by Hewlett-Packard.

Epson probably would have entered the laser printer business eventually. The long-term viability of the dot matrix market was already in

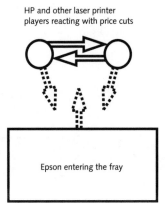

HP and other laser printer
players reacting with price cuts

Epson entering the fray

question. But by doing so aggressively, attacking with a 5 percent discount, Epson triggered a price war that accelerated the decline of the dot matrix printer, effectively pulling the rug out from under itself. Had the company chosen inaction (or at the least, less aggressive action), it might have generated a decreasing, yet attractive, stream of cash flow from its core business and won the time to build up a more viable laser jet business.

THE BENEFITS OF INACTION Inaction can be a powerful and aggressive choice. Intel, for example, is a highly fluid and competitive company. Yet it intentionally holds back from many opportunities in order to avoid competing with customers. It will not, for example, introduce products such as mobile phones or Personal Digital Assistants (PDAs) that depend on Intel chips but that would compete with existing Intel customers.

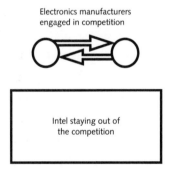

Electronics manufacturers
engaged in competition

Intel staying out of
the competition

Forgoing such tempting opportunities is difficult. A near-term cost-benefit analysis might prove that such a move would create value—i.e., a new Intel-manufactured PDA would generate more profits than Intel would give up in lost customers. But the longer-term lens shows that Intel's policy is highly profitable. Intel remains a trusted supplier of choice for most large electronics companies. Intel may "lose" current battles, such as the PDA battle, but the long-term payoff of steady customer relationships is well worth it.

Virgin Atlantic Airways is another aggressive company willing to hold back. Over the 1990s, it expanded into countries across Asia with a spectrum of ventures ranging from travel (it sold 49 percent of its airline to Singapore Airlines), to retail (it operates more than thirty Virgin Megastores in Japan), to a mobile phone service. It plans to continue this momentum by spinning an expanding web of alliances across South and Southeast Asia. As of the year 2000, it expected half of its value to come from Asia within five years.

Yet despite its aggressive attack on Asia, as of the writing of this book it has left the most promising Asian market—China—untouched. It views China as a high-risk opportunity that it must approach cautiously. Virgin got a taste of the care needed in handling Chinese operations when, in 1998, Richard Branson's hot air balloon strayed into Chinese air space. Branson was attempting a record around-the-world balloon flight. He had permission to fly over part of China but was blown off course into a more central area of China. Chinese officials nearly forced Branson's crew to attempt a risky nighttime landing in Tibet. Branson's attempt was nearly halted at Tibet. High-level, rapid-paced diplomacy between the United Kingdom and China saved Branson's mission in the last minute. But the experience left a mark on Virgin. As Andrew Crassiati, one of Virgin's key executives in Asia, said about China, "We're nervous about not wanting to mess it up." The renegade expansion that characterizes Virgin's expansion in the United Kingdom, Europe, Japan, and South Asia stops abruptly at the Chinese border.

> *The most yielding parts of the world*
> *Overtake the most rigid parts of the world*
> *The insubstantial can penetrate continually.*
> *Therefore I know that without action there is advantage.*
> *This philosophy without words,*

This advantage without action,
It is rare, in the world, to attain them.

—Lao Tzu, *Tao Te Ching*, chapter 43[11]

CAO CAO LETS A FAMILY DESTROY ITSELF In A.D. 200 there was a turning point in the war between Cao Cao and a rival warlord, Yuang Shao. In that year, Cao Cao inflicted a number of victories over Yuang Shao and built momentum that demoralized his opponent. In A.D.202, the shame of constant defeat led Yuang Shao to sickness, then death. He had three sons, all of whom desired to succeed him.

In a break with tradition, the eldest son was passed over, and power was given to the second-eldest son. The youngest son supported this decision. Naturally, the eldest did not. So the Yuang brothers began to fight for control.

Cao Cao saw the brothers' internal conflict as an opportunity, and he attacked. But his threat convinced the Yuang brothers to set aside their quarrels and unify in defense. Cao Cao pulled back from his offensive in order to give the Yuang brothers' conflict more time to gestate. The brothers quickly picked up their differences, which again escalated into battles.

Over the next three years, Cao Cao capitalized on the Yuang brothers' disunity. He picked off four of their provinces and convinced many of the brothers' subjects, including their generals, to defect. But he held off launching a full, direct assault.

By 205, Cao Cao's soldiers attacked and killed the eldest brother. By this time Cao Cao had taken control of a great portion of the Yuang family's territory. The two remaining brothers were forced to flee their kingdom. They found shelter with a nomadic tribe called the Wuhuan. Cao Cao's application of the stratagem *Watch the fire on the other shore* was successful because he had captured all of the Yuang family's territory at minimal cost.

He might have ended his conquest there, but he felt the remaining Yuang brothers still posed a threat. Strains of Yuang loyalty were still woven throughout the populace. If the brothers returned, Cao Cao might face a revolution.

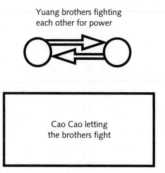

Yuang brothers fighting
each other for power

Cao Cao letting
the brothers fight

Two years later, in 207, Cao Cao attacked the Wuhuan tribe that sheltered the Yuang brothers. After a long march, Cao Cao's troops crushed the Wuhuan and killed the clan's leader. The two Yuang brothers, however, managed to escape. They sought shelter from the leader of a more distant nomadic tribe, Gongsun Kang.

Cao Cao's advisors urged him to continue his pursuit. But Cao Cao calmly declined. He explained that he would simply request Gongsun Kang to deliver the Yuang brothers' heads.

His request to Gongsun Kang was soon answered with the arrival of two boxes. Each contained the head of a Yuang brother.

Cao Cao's advisors eagerly questioned how he knew that Gongsun Kang would grant his request. Cao Cao said, "Gongsun Kang has always been wary of the Yuang tribe. He was afraid [the brothers] might usurp his position . . . If we had pressed them with violent attacks, they would have joined together in defense. But our retreat prompted them to plot against one another."

The first application of *Watch the fire on the other shore* delivered Cao Cao victory over the Yuang brothers' territory. The second application made this victory permanent.

SUMMARY Whether in business or war, inaction is a powerful choice. We should set aside our focus on winning today's war to appreciate the value of inaction today, which can deliver victory tomorrow.

Let the Plum Tree Wither in Place of the Peach

李代桃僵

When loss is inevitable, sacrifice the part for the benefit of the whole.

—FROM *THE 36 STRATAGEMS*

A S A MATTER OF CONVENIENCE and habit, we concentrate on one war at a time. Yet our goals are likely be to longer-term than one war. Our next war may be more important than this one. By losing today to win tomorrow, we can seize advantages that others overlook.

Companies that give up the tendency of focusing on one war at a time may lose one war to win another. Their actions often appear counterintuitive until the next war begins, at which time their actions prove brilliant. This tactic of self-sacrifice is what *The 36 Stratagems* calls *Let the plum tree wither in place of the peach*.

KEY ELEMENTS:

- You cannot win across all wars/fronts

- You allow your adversary victory on one war/front

- You thereby strengthen your ability to win another war/on another front

- You defeat your adversary

Your adversary attacking what you sacrificed

You sacrificing one part ...

... to allow the better part to survive

SACRIFICE AS A PATH TO POWER Competing with Sony can be frustrating. By the time you identify an opening, Sony is already filling it with a substitute product. Sony damages existing sales to preempt competitors from doing so. Although this tactic may be logical, it is counterintuitive, and one that most companies understand but are uncomfortable implementing.

The theory of maximizing profits dictates introducing a new product only when competitors have a superior substitute in hand. Doing so sooner would unnecessarily damage the sales of existing products. Yet Sony regularly introduces new substitutes for existing products in the absence of imminent competitive threats. Why is this?

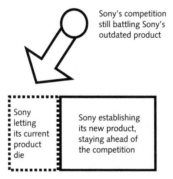

Sony's competition still battling Sony's outdated product

Sony letting its current product die

Sony establishing its new product, staying ahead of the competition

Sony's approach is logical if we shift our view of Sony's business. In particular, if we see Sony's business as a stream of products rather than one product, self-cannibalization becomes an approach to protecting the long-term value of this stream. It may damage the profitability of a single product, but by keeping competition off balance, Sony can increase the value of products two or three iterations into the future. By launching more than eighty models of portable music players in the ten years following the Walkman's introduction, Sony probably sacrificed profits: It replaced versions that still had earning power. But this rapid-fire approach had a longer-term benefit. It complicated competitors' efforts to establish a foothold in the new portable music player segment and thereby helped Sony dominate the segment. Short-term or one-product logic would have ruled out such cannibalism. Following that logic might have cost Sony the dominance it enjoyed for many years.

One might argue that self-cannibalization is a blind habit unique to Sony's culture and that it is therefore not necessarily driven by economic logic. But if this were true, if Sony were simply a rapid innovator, its approach would be consistent across markets and products. Sony's approach is calculated, not habitual, and not consistent. In the high-priced, slower-paced, video game console market, for example, Sony waited six years between product introductions. It similarly varies its innovations by market. It launches more products with smaller changes in Asia and few products with bigger changes in the United States. Sony has built strong positions across many product segments by embracing sacrifice—an approach inconsistent with a "one-war, one-product" view.

BEING THE COMPETITION Following the same logic of Sony—that it's better to steal your own customers than to allow a competitor to do so—Jack Welch, General Electric's CEO, ordered his managers to destroy their businesses in 1999. This was at the height of the Internet revolution. Welch was committed to converting the hundred-plus-year-old company into an e-business. He wanted to wake up managers to the threat that online competitors posed and to ensure that GE preempted all potential attacks.

Each business unit assembled a cross-functional team that for six to eight months dedicated itself to thinking like the competition. They visualized online ventures that eroded their own businesses. Then they built business plans for the most promising ones. This process helped GE identify weaknesses and attack those weaknesses before others could do so.

GE's "destroy your business" effort captivated the press and industry watchers, mainly because it appeared counterintuitive. Why would someone destroy his or her own business? But by taking the longer-term cyclical view of time, in which business is a never-ending game, killing your own business can be logical. If we give up winning today's battle and instead focus on the higher-order goal of winning an endless stream of battles, we can begin to outthink our competition.

THE GENERAL SACRIFICES HIS WORST HORSES During the Warring States period, the royals and generals regularly entertained themselves by gambling on races among their private stocks of horses. The stakes on these races were high.

One day a well-known military advisor and descendant of Sun Tzu named Sun Bin noticed that General Tian Ji was preoccupied. When Sun Bin inquired, the general explained that his horses, which regularly lost, had cost him significant sums of money. Sun Bin offered to accompany the general to the next match to see if he could devise a strategy whereby the general would win. The general gratefully accepted.

At the race match, Sun Bin learned that the races consisted of three heats. The best horses of the contestants competed in the first heat; their second-best horses, in the second; and their worst horses, in the third. He also noticed that the general's horses were in each instance slightly slower than the competition. This was enough information for Sun Bin to devise a strategy that would ensure General Tian Ji victory.

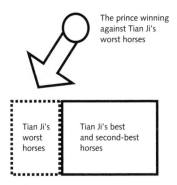

The prince winning against Tian Ji's worst horses

Tian Ji's worst horses

Tian Ji's best and second-best horses

After the races, Sun Bin told General Tian Ji that he had a plan. He suggested that the general call another race and be prepared to bet heavily on it. The general had great confidence in Sun Bin, so he planned a high-profile competition. He invited the prince to compete and thousands of peasants and royal subjects to attend. He put much at risk both financially and in terms of his reputation.

In the first heat, Sun Bin advised the general to race his worst horses against the prince's best. The prince easily defeated the general. The crowd cheered; the prince smiled confidently, but Sun Bin remained calm.

In the second heat, Sun Bin advised the general to race his best horses against the prince's second-best horses. The general's best horses, although no match for the prince's best horses, easily defeated the prince's second-best horses. The score was tied one to one.

In the final, deciding race, the general ran his second-best horses against the prince's worst horses and won. By sacrificing his worst horses, General Tian Ji won the tournament and recouped a large share of his losses.

> *The strategy of guerrilla warfare is manifestly unlike that employed in orthodox operations, as the basic tactic of the former is constant activity and movement. There is in guerrilla warfare no such thing as a decisive battle.*

MAO TSE-TUNG, *ON GUERILLA WARFARE*[iii]

SUMMARY This tactic of sacrifice, of losing today to win tomorrow, has served some of history's most powerful generals and today's most powerful companies. Whether dealing with horse races, wars, or business conflicts, broadening our objectives beyond the current war frees us to seize opportunities that our adversaries cannot see. Tian Ji's willingness to give up near-term gambling profits and Sony and GE's willingness to give up near-term business profits revealed new opportunities.

The Stratagem of the Open City Gates

空城計

In spite of the inferiority of your force, deliberately make your defensive line defenseless in order to confuse the enemy. In situations when the enemies are many and you are few, this tactic seems all the more intriguing.

—FROM *THE 36 STRATAGEMS*

O UR COMPETITORS study us carefully, trying to assess our threat and anticipate our moves. In response, we go to great lengths to keep information hidden. Indeed, our commitment to protecting internal information is so pervasive that an entire industry—competitive intelligence—has flourished around it.

Yet one of the most successful business moves begins with revealing, rather than hiding, information. A carefully staged peek into our strategies, intentions, or capabilities can influence our competitors' actions and deliver an advantage to us.

KEY ELEMENTS:

- Your adversary is attacking or preparing to attack

- You reveal your strength or weakness

- Your adversary calls off his attack, because he fears your strength or no longer considers you a threat

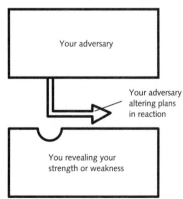

Your adversary

Your adversary altering plans in reaction

You revealing your strength or weakness

WHEN STRONG A company regarded as a tough competitor can scare away opposition simply by making noise during its approach. Microsoft's worldwide reputation as aggressive, persistent, and usually successful is the weapon the company wields to clear away potential opponents. When Microsoft announces its intention to introduce a new product or enter a new market, would-be competitors recalculate their projections. Investors readjust their risk assessments. Customers rethink their purchases and consider waiting for the Microsoft product. In other words, when Microsoft announces it is entering a new segment, the market makes room. If Microsoft hid its intentions, it would have to spend more to win over customers and investors.

Microsoft implements this tactic intentionally and proactively. It does not depend on the market to link past successes to future success. It makes this linkage explicit.

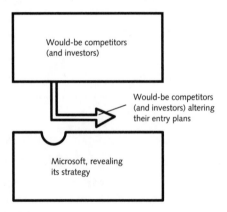

In revealing Microsoft's "digital home" strategy, which envisions home appliances (e.g., refrigerators, televisions, and systems such as alarms and lighting) networked through Microsoft products, Bill Gates said, "The way you get to our vision [of the digital home] is by building individual products that are the best in their own categories. It's like Microsoft Office. We built that with Word being the best, Excel being the best. They all had to be the best before the whole integration thing came together."[iv] In other words: Competitors, beware.

Microsoft is not the only company to rely on this stratagem. Any company with a strong reputation for aggressive, competitive practices—such as Gillette, Anheuser-Busch, and Emerson Electric—benefits from revealing its intentions.

WHEN WEAK Weak companies also benefit from revealing their strategies. "Judo economics," a term coined by economists Judith Gelman and Steven Salop in the early 1980s, describes this phenomenon.

The logic behind judo economics is fairly simple. Consider a hypothetical situation: An incumbent happily dominates its market for years until one day a new, smaller attacker gets interested and decides to enter this market. The attacker can enter either aggressively (at a low price and with significant capacity) or timidly (at the same price and/or with limited capacity). Which should it choose?

If the attacker enters the market aggressively with, say, a 20 percent discount and the capacity to serve the entire market, the incumbent will be forced to cut prices and drive the attacker out. The incumbent's choices are (a) drop prices and stay in business or (b) keep prices unchanged, lose the entire market, and close down the business. The incumbent must choose (a).

However, if the attacker only has the capacity to serve, say, 10 percent of the market, the incumbent would be better off leaving prices unchanged and letting the attacker take its 10 percent. The incumbent's choices are (a) drop prices by 20 percent (to match the attacker) and thereby decrease sales by 20 percent across the board or (b) hold prices, lose 10 percent of the market, and thereby decrease sales by 10 percent. The incumbent will choose (b).

So, by revealing a weakness (i.e., its ability to serve only 10 percent of the market), an attacker can ward off retaliation by an incumbent. Of course, further expansion may be in its plans once the attacker has established a stronghold, as was the case for Japanese carmakers entering the United States.

Following the principle of judo economics, Virgin, one of the most aggressive companies of its time, toned down its characteristically grand aspirations when it launched Virgin Cola in the United States. Alexis Dormandy, vice president of operations for Virgin Cola U.S.A., said, "We're here to take on Coke and Pepsi, even if we only get a little corner of the market."[v]

Similarly, in 1992, Kiwi Airlines managed how incumbents in its new market would measure the threat of Kiwi's launch. Commenting on Kiwi's strategy, CEO Robert Iverson said, "We designed our system to stay out of the way of large carriers and to make sure they understand that we pose no threat . . . Kiwi intends to capture, at most, only a 10 percent share of any one market—or no more than four flights per day."[vi]

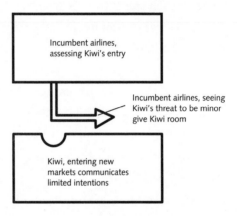

USING WEAKNESS TO COMMUNICATE STRENGTH During the Three Kingdoms period (A.D. 220–265), while the kingdoms of Shu and Wei were at war, the prime minister of Shu found himself in an apparently helpless predicament. Taking a break from fighting, he retired to his base city. He sent most of his troops off to battle and ordered half of the remaining troops to leave the city to help move supplies in another town. This left him with just 2,500 troops.

The news of an approaching Wei army, 150,000 soldiers strong, came too late for the prime minister to call back his men. He would have to work with what he had.

His two obvious choices were to flee or to fight, each of which meant death for him and his subjects. The Wei army outnumbered his by a ratio of sixty to one. If he fought, he would lose. If he fled, the Wei would hunt him down and kill him. The situation's helplessness made his subjects faint, but the prime minister remained calm. He had a stratagem in mind.

As great clouds of dust signaled the approach of the Wei army, the prime minister ordered his soldiers to occupy their posts as normal, threatening to behead anyone who attempted escape. He then had the city gates opened, and he placed twenty soldiers at each gate.

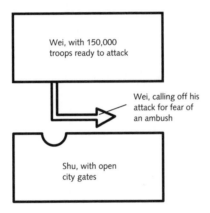

Dressed as civilians, the soldiers pretended to sweep the streets. Finally, he ascended an observation post, carrying incense and a zither. He lit the incense and calmly played the zither.

Wei scouts were shocked at the strange signs of calm in Shu's city. When they reported that the city gates were open, civilians were sweeping the streets, and guards were at their usual posts, the Wei general was incredulous. He mounted a horse to inspect the scene himself. He too found the same signs of calm. Then, when he heard the prime minister playing serene songs on a zither without a hint of fear in his voice despite the presence of 150,000 troops at his doorstep, the general concluded that the prime minister had set a trap. He explained to his advisors that the prime minister was known for being conservative and careful, and he would not take such a bold position without a powerful stratagem in hand. Wei turned his troops around and left.

Thus, Shu's prime minister saved his life and his city. He forced 150,000 enemy troops to retreat with only 2,500 soldiers, open city gates, and a zither.

> *"Things pass for what they seem, not for what they are. Only rarely do people look into them, and many are satisfied with appearances."*
>
> —BALTASAR GRACIAN, *THE ART OF WORLDLY WISDOM*[vii]

SUMMARY Like Microsoft and Kiwi Airlines, Shu simply allowed his adversary a peek behind his city walls. By carefully revealing our strength, strategy, or (in the case of Shu) our level of concern, we shape our adversary's perception of his situation. This determines his actions, and in turn, influences our chances of success.

Await the Exhausted Enemy
At Your Ease

以逸待勞

To weaken the enemy, it is not necessary to attack him directly.
Tire him by carrying out an active defense and in so doing his strength
will be reduced and your side will gain the upper hand.

—FROM *THE 36 STRATAGEMS*

WE EXPECT COMPETITION to be contained within defined boundaries. For the most part, these boundaries hold: Television networks battle for consumers within the boundaries of the living room and cereal manufacturers do battle within the walls of grocery stores.

Occasionally, however, our battles break out of their borders. Such "new game" events shift power, often humbling long-dominant incumbents and crowning young challengers. Surviving such "new game" shifts is difficult because competitiveness on today's battlefield will not guarantee competitiveness on tomorrow's. Predicting these shifts is also difficult because they happen so rarely. But by pretending such shifts will not happen, as we often do, we rule out any chance of success or advantage these shifts might offer.

Clever companies and armies have toppled more-powerful adversaries by predicting the battleground to which their conflict would shift, setting up a position there, and waiting for their adversary to approach.

KEY ELEMENTS:

- You predict that the battleground will shift

- You set up a defendable position on the new battleground

- You wait for your adversary

- When your adversary arrives, you use your superior position to defeat him

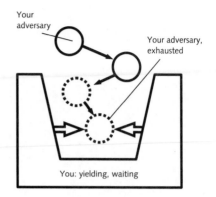

Because we view confrontation as temporary or close-ended, we expect it to remain within defined boundaries. In fact, our first step in assessing a competitive situation is to define the market, which is to define the boundaries within which we plan to battle our competitors.

For the most part, these boundaries hold. Television networks battle predominantly in living rooms; cereal manufacturers, in grocery stores. These boundaries have not changed measurably in decades. Indeed, battles rarely break through their boundaries within the battles' "lifetimes." When they do, we call them "new games" and deal with them as unpredictable innovations that damage some companies, kill others, and reward still others. When consumers broke the boundaries of their purchasing behavior by leaving the city to shop in the suburbs, most retailers lost ground. They had defined their battleground by the rigid boundaries of the city. They had not contemplated fighting in the suburbs. So when the action shifted, they were unprepared. Many risked losing their business as a result, and many did.

Surviving such events is difficult, since competitiveness on today's battlefield does not guarantee competitiveness tomorrow; battlefield shifts are difficult to predict. But by pretending such shifts will not happen, we rule out any chance of success that we might have or advantage that we might capture. Seeing our game as unbounded overcomes this dilemma.

Battleground shifts become inevitable if we extend what we typically define as a conflict's "lifetime"—if we view business as an endless war, a never-ending stream of battles. "New games" become continuations of old games. They transform the inexplicable blips we live with to something we can plan for and on which we can capitalize. Indeed, long-term success depends on predicting and capitalizing on "new games."

As the following cases will show, companies have turned battleground shifts into advantages, overcoming even their largest competitors by identifying new battlegrounds; setting up a defensive position there; and waiting for their competition.

> *One who takes position first at the battleground and awaits the enemy is at ease.*
>
> *One who takes position later at the battleground and hastens to do battle is at labor.*
>
> *Thus one skilled at battle summons others and is not summoned by them.*
>
> —SUN TZU, *THE ART OF WAR*[viii]

WAL-MART AWAITS ITS EXHAUSTED COMPETITION In 1945, the company that was to become Wal-Mart consisted of one variety store in Newport, Arkansas. In just over thirty years, it became the largest retailer in the world, with more than 3,000 stores in all fifty U.S. states and with operations in Argentina, Brazil, Canada, China, Germany, South Korea, Mexico, and the United Kingdom. Wal-Mart owes much of its success to a simple tactic: identifying the next battleground, setting up a stronghold there, and waiting for the competition.

When Wal-Mart began its national expansion in the early 1970s, large retailers such as Sears, JCPenny, and Kmart positioned stores only in large city and town centers. Wal-Mart took the opposite approach: It focused on smaller towns, in part to avoid direct competition and in part because it believed the battleground would shift. As Wal-Mart's founder Sam Walton explained,

> [Our strategy] was simply to put good-sized discount stores into little one-horse towns, which everyone else was ignoring. In those days Kmart wasn't going into towns below 50,000 and even Gibson wouldn't go to towns much smaller that 10,000 or 12,000. We knew our formula was working even in towns smaller than 5,000 people, and there were plenty of those towns out there for us to expand into. When people want to simplify the Wal-Mart story that is usually how they sum up the secret of our success: "Oh, they went into small towns when nobody else would."[ix]

Companies that avoid direct competition simply to reduce the cost of battle risk holding a big piece of an insignificant pie. But Wal-Mart was doing more than avoiding direct competition—it was betting that the battleground would move toward small towns and suburbs.

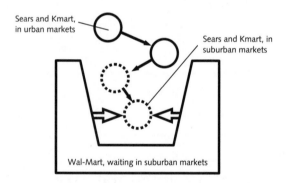

For reasons still in contention, consumers migrated to suburban neighborhoods and increasingly preferred suburban to city-center retail stores. Leading retailers faced with declining sales in their key locations followed customers into these smaller markets. When they got there, however, they encountered an unexpectedly strong competitor.

Wal-Mart had been waiting for them, fortified with a strong brand and an efficient distribution system. The advantage Sears possessed in serving large urban centers did not carry into Wal-Mart's backyard. Sears fell from Wal-Mart leader to Wal-Mart follower, and it still has not caught up.

ASAHI WAITS FOR KIRIN AT THE SUPERMARKET In the late 1980s, Japan's Asahi Breweries predicted a shift in consumer buying habits. It capitalized on this foresight in the same way Wal-Mart had: Asahi established a stronghold on the new battleground and waited for its competition.

Asahi aspired to overtake the leading Japanese brewery, Kirin. But winning shelf space was extremely difficult because Kirin's influence over liquor stores, through which most Japanese consumers purchased beer, was too strong. Luckily, Asahi saw consumer purchasing behavior changing. Women were buying more beer, for one thing, and because they preferred supermarkets to liquor stores, beer sales increased in supermarkets. Asahi believed and bet that supermarkets would eventually overshadow liquor stores to become the most important beer channel. It

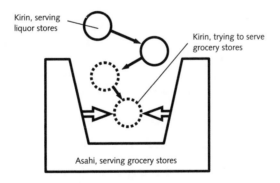

stopped banging its head against liquor stores and instead developed strong distribution relationships with key grocers.

Asahi's prognostication proved correct. The trend toward grocery stores continued. Eventually Kirin caught on and tried to followed beer drinkers into supermarkets, just as Sears had tried to follow its consumers into the suburbs. And just as Sears was taken by surprise by an unexpectedly strong Wal-Mart, Kirin found Asahi, with its supermarket relationships and expertise, a superior competitor. Asahi's ambush turned the tables on Kirin and gave Asahi the leading position in the Japanese beer market.

LURING AN ADVERSARY WITH CAMPFIRES In 342 B.C., three states engaged in war: Wei, Qi, and Han. Wei attacked Han. While Wei was besieging Han, Han asked the state of Qi for help. Qi prepared its army and began marching to the capital of Wei to implement the stratagem *Besiege Wei to rescue Zhao* (see Stratagem 7), just as Chi had done to Wei twelve years earlier. The goal was to force Wei to return to defend the capital and call off its attack on Han.

Remembering the painful consequences of falling for the stratagem *Besiege Wei to rescue Zhao*, the Wei army, under the leadership of General Pang Juan, pulled back its troops. They rushed home to defend their capital against Qi's attack.

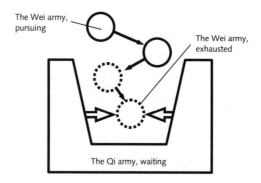

The Wei army, pursuing

The Wei army, exhausted

The Qi army, waiting

But Sun Bin, the leader of the Qi army, had a new stratagem in mind. He knew that Pang Juan underestimated the Qi army. So rather than attack the Wei capital, he feigned a retreat. He used a creative ploy to lure Pang Juan out of the capital. During the first night of his retreat he had his army light 100,000 campfires. During the second night, his soldiers lit 50,000, and on the third night, only 30,000.

Pang Juan read this as a sign that the Qi army was dwindling. Tasting an easy victory, he took pursuit. He gathered a collection of lightly armed troops and marched them rapidly, at twice the normal speed, toward the retreating Qi army.

Sun Bin calculated that at dawn Pang Juan would reach a town called Maling. He set up an ambush there, and he waited.

The Wei troops arrived on schedule but exhausted from their strenuous march. Sun Bin's army, which was rested, fortified, and three times the size Pang Juan expected, easily defeated the Wei troops. Pang Juan committed suicide on the battlefield. Sun Bin had identified the next battleground; fortified his troops there; and forced his adversary to exhaust itself getting there.

SUMMARY Insight gave Qi the same advantage that enabled Wal-Mart and Asahi to topple their dominant adversaries. It allowed each to turn battleground shifts into advantages by identifying new battlegrounds, setting up a defensive position there, and waiting. If we take a short-term view, attaining such insights seems difficult because battleground shifts appear to be once-in-a-lifetime occurrences. But taking a long-term view often makes such insight attainable. What appears a "new game" on a 10-year scale may be but a blip on a 100-year scale.

Exchange the Role of Guest for That of Host

反客為主

Whenever there is a chance, enter into the decision-making body of your ally and extend your influence skillfully step-by-step. Eventually, put it under your control.

—FROM *THE 36 STRATAGEMS*

I F OUR GOALS extend beyond the immediate battle, it becomes accept-able to open with a seemingly weak move. A deceptively weak move can serve as a foot in the door that creates an opportunity to infiltrate our adversary and take control. The acceptance of our inferior position acts as our Trojan horse.

This tactic has delivered well-known corporate power reversals. Take the cases of both Microsoft and Intel. They were born as subordinate suppliers to IBM. Now they both command more power than their former sponsor. The convenience store chain, 7–11 Japan, originated as a subsidiary of the U.S.-based 7–11 chain, but now it owns 70 percent of its "parent."

The pattern Wal-Mart, IBM, Intel, and 7–11 Japan each followed—building on a position of weakness to capture control—is what *The 36 Stratagems* calls *Exchange the role of guest for that of host.*

KEY ELEMENTS:

- Your adversary accepts you as unthreatening

- You incrementally build power over your adversary

- You take control

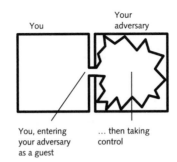

You

Your adversary

You, entering your adversary as a guest

... then taking control

FROM BUYER TO BOSS Wal-Mart offers consumers superior value. It can sell products at lower prices than its competition without forfeiting quality. This unique ability has fueled Wal-Mart's incessant growth and seemingly insurmountable competitiveness. The retailer has been able to do what its competitors cannot primarily because it is able to cut costs out of the supply chain and thereby reduce the costs of the goods it sells. It squeezes the margins of all players in its supply chain from raw material suppliers to manufacturers. To push down manufacturers' margins, Wal-Mart adopts the tactic of *Exchanging the role of guest for that of host.*

An Asian apparel manufacturer shared his experience of working with Wal-Mart. He described a process Wal-Mart has repeated with other manufacturers throughout the region. The process overcomes the initial resistance that manufacturers often have to working with Wal-Mart which, they think, allows manufacturers to earn only extremely low margins.

First, Wal-Mart places a relatively small order that the manufacturer eagerly accepts, because such a small order does not make the manufacturer dependent on Wal-Mart. Wal-Mart then requests additional capacity that the manufacturer almost always grants. The manufacturer would rather give any extra capacity it has to Wal-Mart instead of investing the time in winning a new customer. The manufacturer's rationale is, "You already have a buyer waiting; why would you waste time hunting down another buyer?" So Wal-Mart's share of the manufacturer's sales have grown from an insignificant 10 percent to a slightly more significant 15 percent.

This development in isolation does not at first noticeably shift the balance of power between Wal-Mart and its manufacturer. But Wal-Mart repeats this process a few times, incrementally growing its share of the manufacturer's production. During this "infiltration" period, Wal-Mart demands good, but not overly aggressive, prices from the manufacturer. The manufacturer finds it difficult to turn away Wal-Mart's easy business.

After some time, Wal-Mart comes to represent a significant share of the manufacturer's capacity. Wal-Mart then begins demanding deeper discounts. The manufacturer must now choose between cutting margins and losing a large customer, perhaps its largest at this point. The manufacturer naturally acquiesces and cuts margins.

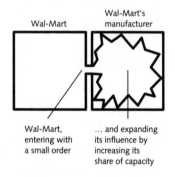

Wal-Mart

Wal-Mart's manufacturer

Wal-Mart, entering with a small order

... and expanding its influence by increasing its share of capacity

Interestingly, by cutting margins, the manufacturer increases its dependence on Wal-Mart. With lower margins, maintaining high utilization levels (i.e., keeping their machines working) becomes more critical to profitability. So when capacity becomes available, the manufacturer is motivated to sell it quickly; Wal-Mart, with its vast retail network, is the customer most likely to buy extra capacity quickly.

Wal-Mart's process turns an initially weak position into one of dominance. By opening with a seemingly innocuous position and then building dependence incrementally, the company effectively reduces manufacturer resistance. This tactic is central to Wal-Mart's overall success.

Manufacturer dependence allows Wal-Mart to demand low margins and therefore sell at lower prices than its competitors.

FROM GUEST TO GOVERNOR Xiang Liang descended from a long line of generals. However, when his home state, Chu, fell to the powerful Qin dynasty, his family lost power. Even before this happened, however, as a youth Xiang Liang murdered a man and fled his home with his nephew, Xiang Yu. They took up asylum in the state of Wu. This is how it came to be that a man destined to lead armies became a lowly administrator, an exile, and an unwilling citizen of the oppressive Qin dynasty. He was, naturally, hungry for change.

Xiang Liang developed a reputation as a strong administrator and leader. The governor of Wu, who had granted Xiang Liang and his nephew asylum, grew to trust them. Over the years, Xiang Liang patiently climbed up Wu's organizational rungs. He became a valued advisor to the governor.

In 209 B.C., when states and kingdoms throughout the Qin dynasty ignited in revolt, the governor of Wu turned to Xiang Liang. He wanted his state to join the revolt, and asked Xiang Liang and his nephew to lead an army.

Xiang Liang saw this as an opportunity to complete his ascent of Wu's governing ladder and take control. He asked to confer with his nephew before accepting the challenge. But the plan he and his nephew devised was not what the governor expected.

Xiang Liang and Xiang Yu

The Wu governor

Uncle and nephew, receiving asylum

... then expanding their influence, ultimately taking control

After Xiang Liang and his nephew jointly accepted the governor's challenge, the three men met to discuss how Wu should join the revolution. In the middle of this meeting, Xiang Liang gave his nephew a secret cue. Without warning or hesitation, his nephew, Xiang Yu, drew his sword and beheaded the governor. Xiang Liang then took the state seals and declared himself governor. To quell the opposition, Xiang Yu swiftly killed any objecting onlookers.

The uncle-nephew team continued their ascent of power. They joined the revolution and won many battles, including the battle for their home state, Chu. Xiang Liang became a contender for the reconquered Chu throne but for political reasons could not secure it. He died in battle soon afterward. Xiang Yu became a contender for the entire dynasty but suffered a similar fate, dying in battle before the dynasty's next ruler was named.

The asylum seekers exchanged their roles from guests to governor. They almost continued their rise to become king and emperor. Their success lay in timing. By accepting seemingly powerless positions as lowly administrators, they placed their feet into the door of power. By taking small steps, none of which warranted suspicion, they infiltrated their adversary. Once they had built sufficient trust and dependence, they took control.

> *Make people depend on you. . . . You will get more from dependence than*
> *from courtesy. He who has already drunk turns his back on the well, and*
> *the orange already squeezed turns from gold into mud.*

—BALTASAR GRACIAN, *THE ART OF WORLDLY WISDOM*[x]

SUMMARY By taking power incrementally, we blur the line between passive and aggressive and so prevent our adversaries from raising their defenses. Because our adversaries are thinking about today's battle while we are planning for tomorrow's, they are comforted by their current success and therefore fail to prepare for our incursion. This stratagem requires that we be willing to take an inferior position today, as Wal-Mart does with its manufacturers and as Xiang Liang did with the governor of Wu, in exchange for a superior position in the future.

> *For such a prince cannot rely upon what he observes in quiet times, when citizens had need of the state, because then every one agrees with him; they all promise, and when death is far distant they all wish to die for him; but in troubled times, when the state has need of its citizens, then he finds but few. . . . Therefore, a wise prince ought to adopt such a course that his citizens will always in every sort and kind of circumstance have need of the state and of him, and then he will always find them faithful.*
>
> —NICOLO MACHIAVELLI, *THE PRINCE*[xi]

Borrow the Road
to Conquer Gao

假道伐虢

When a small state, located between two big states,
is being threatened by the enemy state, you should immediately send troops
to rescue it, thereby expanding your sphere of influence. Mere talk
cannot win the trust of a state in a difficult position.

—FROM *THE 36 STRATAGEMS*

WE TEND TO VIEW ALLIANCES as roads of hope with uncertain ends. We take our partners' hands and jointly follow these roads, hoping they will last but uncertain as to where they will lead. Although we contemplate at length the consequences of an unsuccessful alliance ending (e.g., our agreements are filled with provisions that dictate rights and responsibilities if the alliance fails), we rarely contemplate the end of a successful alliance. Indeed, we consider a successful alliance one that never ends.

Another view is that of the alliance as a borrowed road. This suggests that the road does have a certain end. In fact, the stratagem *Borrow the road to conquer Gao* recommends that our actual goals lie beyond this end and that our alliance is temporary—a borrowed road—to achieve these goals. Companies that have most benefited from alliances often embrace this view.

KEY ELEMENTS:

- You share a common objective or enemy with another

- You form an alliance to achieve this objective

- You then take your ally

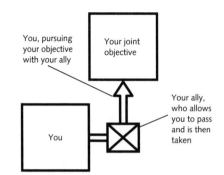

BORROWING TO BUILD AN ADVANTAGE In 1984, with $80,000 in seed funding, Liu Chuanzhi created a company with a vague mission: to commercialize technology developed by the Chinese Academy of Sciences. Over the next several years, the company, Legend, evolved into an average member of China's legion of domestic computer firms. Because the government would not grant Legend the authority to manufacture its own computers, Legend was relegated to distributing computers and related hardware for international manufacturers.

Legend, however, was learning. It would drain experience out of its partners and then build a formidable advantage. It was borrowing a road that would convert its inauspicious beginning into a story of great success.

Legend became, and has remained, the largest distributor of Hewlett-Packard (HP) computers and Toshiba notebooks in China. In this role, the company absorbed HP's practices. It simultaneously developed a unique understanding of how to serve Chinese consumers. For example, it created a breakthrough keyboard that facilitated writing Chinese characters; and, because Chinese consumers are less familiar with computers than are United States and European consumers, it ran computer education road shows countrywide. In addition, the company established an enviable distribution network comprising more than 2,000 distributors.

HP and Toshiba partnerships afforded Legend a valuable foundation of best management practices, customer understanding, and distribution infrastructure that enabled the company to decisively beat rivals during the early 1990s. However, this changed in 1992 when China lowered import restrictions. Foreign firms rushed in and quickly cut down local computer companies' collective market share to 30 percent from 70 percent.

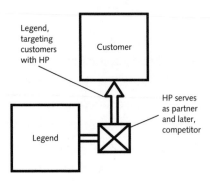

Legend, which had begun manufacturing its own branded computers, and still had a substantial distribution business, thrived under the pressure. Following U.S. practices, it took the radical move of offering shares in the company to the employees. This helped to attract top talent. It funneled its commercial and technological knowledge (borrowed from its alliances with HP and other foreign firms, including Intel), into the effort to become a highly competitive computer manufacturer. So while other Chinese computer firms retreated or closed down, Legend's share grew. It reached 5 percent in 1995, from close to zero, and continued to grow. In 1998, it captured 14 percent of the market, making it the top-selling brand. Today, it commands about 30 percent, outselling international leaders such as IBM, HP, and Compaq by impressive margins.

Legend owes a debt of gratitude to its partners for much of its success. Liu Chuanzhi said, "Our earliest and best teacher was Hewlett-Packard."[xii]

HP concurs. HP executive Ken Koo says, "Legend grew with us. They learned vendor channel management from HP. We helped develop Legend into a strong PC company in China."xiii

A UNIVERSAL TACTIC Some businesspeople first introduced to this tactic shy away from it, questioning its ethical grounds. Yet many of the most competitive companies throughout the world follow this temporary alliance pattern to build advantage. DHL, for example, partnered with its Chinese equivalent, Sinotrans, to build a network in China. It later used its resulting Chinese operations to compete directly with its former partner. U.S. firms eagerly partnered with Komatsu, the Japanese heavy machinery manufacturer, despite being clear that Komatsu was seeking to build know-how that it would later use against its arch rival, Caterpillar.

A DEPOSIT OF JADE In 658 B.C., the duke of Jin was contemplating how to continue expanding his state. He had, over the years, overtaken many other states and now enjoyed great power. He was particularly concentrating on two smaller states that bordered his own: Yu and Gao, which anticipated the duke's ambitions and so fortified their Jin borders. They recognized an informal pact they had to support each other in case of an attack. As a result of this coordination, a successful incursion would cost the duke considerable resources.

One of the duke's generals suggested that if the duke could attack one of the small states through the other, his chances of success would be greatly improved, because their common borders were not heavily guarded. He proposed that the duke bribe Yu's leader, who was known to be greedy, with lavish gifts in exchange for passage through Yu to attack Gao. The duke countered that the cost might not be worth the gain. The general responded that the duke should think of the bribes as deposits, not gifts. Once successful, the duke could withdraw his bribes from Yu's stores again.

The duke agreed to the plan. He offered Yu's leader fine horses and jade in exchange for passage. An advisor to Yu's leader counseled him not to accept the gifts. "You have heard the saying, 'without lips, the teeth

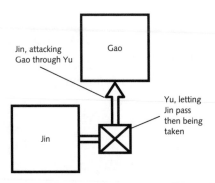

would get cold,'" he said. "Gao and Yu are close neighbors and depend on each other for protection. Without Gao, Yu might not survive. Why should we let Jin pass?" But Yu's leader ignored the warning. He accepted the gifts and let the Jin army pass through his territory to attack Gao.

Gao fell easily to Jin's superior forces. The Jin army, on its way home, attacked and conquered Yu, also relatively quickly. The Jin general took back his duke's jade and horses from Yu's stores and returned them to the duke.

Through a temporary alliance, the duke of Jin upset his opponents' balance and overwhelmed them in succession, conquering both at minimal cost.

SUMMARY Social rules require that we enter alliances as a marriage, without intending on an end. Yet highly competitive companies regularly view alliances as a borrowed road. Just as the duke of Jin did 2,700 years ago, companies such as Legend, DHL, and Komatsu have benefited not from achieving joint objectives through their alliances but rather from pursuing more selfish objectives, such as gaining experience from the temporary ally, or entering into a new market.

And here it is to be noted that a prince ought to take care never to make an alliance with one more powerful than himself for the purpose of attacking others, unless necessity compels him, . . . because if he conquers you, you are at his discretion, and princes ought to avoid as much as possible being at the discretion of any one.

—NICOLO MACHIAVELLI, *THE PRINCE*[xiv]

Shed Your Skin Like the Golden Secada

金蟬脫殼

*Make your front array appear as if you are still holding your position
so that the allied force will not suspect your intention and the enemy troops will not
dare to attack rashly. Then withdraw your main forces secretly.*

—FROM *THE 36 STRATAGEMS*

A CYCLICAL VIEW OF TIME makes it easier for us to accept loss today in exchange for gain tomorrow. This is playing with gain and loss across the dimension of time. We can similarly play with gain and loss across other dimensions, such as markets and businesses. By linking businesses and shifting earnings, a company can manipulate competition and protect profitability.

This is like playing with the good and bad, the hard and the soft ground, in warfare. The key is to look at the whole, not the parts, and while letting your adversary focus on a part and not the whole.

KEY ELEMENTS:

- You establish a façade

- Your adversary focuses on your façade, confusing it for the real action

- You move the real action somewhere else

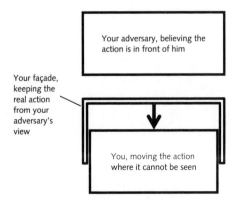

Your adversary, believing the action is in front of him

Your façade, keeping the real action from your adversary's view

You, moving the action where it cannot be seen

Attain both hard and soft.
This is the pattern of Earth.

—SUN TZU, *THE ART OF WAR*[xv]

HOLLOW PROFITS The charter airline business is ruthless. It punishes with losses any airline that fails to achieve 70 percent utilization. Keeping planes full, however, is a challenge. Charter airlines have few means, other than price, by which to differentiate their services and maintain high utilization rates. Passengers rarely can choose which particular charter airline to fly, so branding doesn't help. Rather, institutions, such as tour operators and corporations, make buying decisions. They do not care about the airline's name or the details of its frequent flyer program, but they do care about safety. Regulation ensures airlines' records for safety remain similar, making it almost impossible for airlines to differentiate along this dimension. As a result, airlines are relegated to competing on price alone. Performance, to a great extent, depends on factors outside of their control, such as macroeconomic trends.

The payoff for filling planes, however, is attractive. Revenue from each passenger above minimum utilization represents pure profit because carrying that additional passenger requires no meaningful additional cost.

The Thomson Travel Group of the United Kingdom, for one, has assembled a system to influence the odds of its charter airline gamble. It beats the system by applying a clever stratagem to practically ensure full planes.

Thomson operates three related businesses. Its retail business, Lunn Poly, sells consumers travel services, such as hotel rooms, flights, and tour packages. Its tour operator, Thomson Holidays, packages and manages tours. Thomson's third business is a charter airline, Britannia.

While the three businesses are independent, they can coordinate their efforts to achieve an advantage that competitors cannot. For example, Lunn Poly does not exclusively sell Thomson Holidays' tour packages, but it sends a lot of business to this sister company. Thomson Holidays, in turn, sends much of its business to Britannia, who, in turn, benefits from well-utilized planes.

The impact of this structure is compelling. Thomson's retail and tour businesses make little profit. Indeed, few companies in these markets do. In forgoing retail and tour profits, Thomson benefits in two

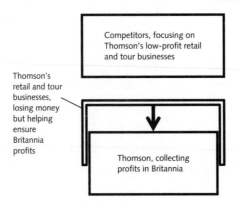

ways. First, it wards off travel retail and tour competitors with low prices and low profitability that diminish would-be competitors' appetites. Second, by ushering customers into Britannia planes, ensuring high utilization, the company can generate abnormally high charter airline profits. Thomson's retail and tour businesses serve as a conduit for the air charter business but also act as a façade that dissuades the competition while the real action takes place elsewhere: Britannia earns unusually high profits.

THE FALSE KING Xiang Yu, who collaborated with his uncle, Xiang Liang, to apply the stratagem *Exchange the role of guest for that of host* and take control of Wu (see Stratagem 23), continued his quest to take down the Han empire. He and his uncle successfully took control of their home state of Chu. Xiang Liang died later during a mission to expand the revolution, and Xiang Yu became warlord of Wu. In this position, Xiang Yu led many successful battles against the king of Han, Gaozu.

After one such battle in the early second century B.C., Gaozu retreated with a diminished army to regroup in a fortified city. However, Xiang Yu followed, surrounded the city, and prepared to finally defeat his archrival.

Gaozu's situation looked dire. But one of his generals proposed a maneuver to allow Gaozu to escape. The general proposed that he pose as the king, focus their adversary's attention on him by feigning a surrender, while the real king, Gaozu, escaped through a side exit of the city. The general was offering his life to save his king. The king accepted.

The general had 2,000 women dress as soldiers. Just before dawn, these women exited the main gate and took up battle formation. Xiang Yu's army reacted quickly. They assembled in formation and prepared for what they hoped would be the final confrontation. But just before daybreak, when the fighting would commence, the general appeared from within the city walls disguised as the king and signaled surrender. His people had run out of food, he explained.

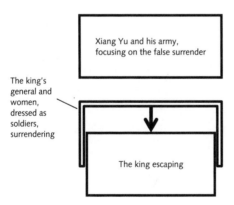

Xiang Yu's soldiers celebrated their long-awaited victory in a joyous uproar. They did not yet realize that who they thought was the king was actually a general, and who they thought were soldiers were actually women in disguise. Under the cover of this façade, with thirty horsemen, Gaozu quietly exited the city through the West gate.

The general's carriage slowly moved toward Xiang Yu. The king was to surrender in person. When Xiang Yu recognized the general and realized he had been tricked, he grew furious. When he learned that a group of horsemen had snuck out of the city and escaped, he had the general burned to death. Gaozu, the king of Han, was saved.

SUMMARY For millennia, leaders have leveraged the tactic of creating a façade to hide the real action occurring somewhere else to overcome adversaries. Companies do this as well by, for example, linking businesses and pooling profits where they incite less competition.

The Stratagem of Injuring Yourself

苦肉計

People rarely inflict injuries on themselves, so when they get injured, it is usually
genuine. Exploit this naivety to make the enemy believe your words; then sowing
discord within the enemy will work. In this case, one takes advantage of the enemy's
weakness, and makes the enemy look as if he were a naive child easily taken.

—FROM *THE 36 STRATAGEMS*

M ANY OF TODAY's most powerful companies grew from positions
of self-imposed weakness. They injured themselves to appear less
threatening, and thereby pacified the opposition, and then built their
power within this protective sphere.

KEY ELEMENTS:

- Your adversary's suspicion
  hinders your success

- You injure yourself to either
  (1) win your adversary's trust
  or (2) avoid appearing to
  be a threat

- Your adversary accepts you
  or lets down his guard

- You take advantage of this
  opening by attacking your
  adversary

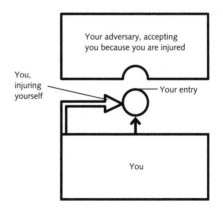

The yielding can triumph over the inflexible;
The weak can triumph over the strong.
Fish should not be taken from deep waters;
Nor should organizations make obvious their advantages.

—LAO TZU, *TAO TE CHING*[xvi]

IBM ACCEPTS A WEAKENED INTEL In the late 1970s, IBM was unsure whether to use Intel's new 8086 microprocessor in the heart of its first PC. IBM dominated the computer industry, but it still worried about whether relying on one supplier for such a critical component might threaten its position. So it asked Intel to license its technology to competitors.

Intel had two options. In the first, it could turn down IBM's request. This carried with it the risk of losing its biggest customer and potentially missing out on the emerging PC sector. But if this approach were

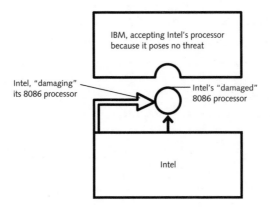

successful—if IBM built its PC around Intel technology—it would provide an enviable payoff: exclusivity. Intel's second option was to accept IBM's request and license Intel's 8086 technology to competitors. This carried less risk (i.e., it nearly guaranteed IBM would adopt the 8086), but forfeited significant profits because competitors would be free to compete with Intel using Intel technology.

The right option depended on what game Intel was playing. If Intel was playing for today's battle, the 8086 microprocessor game, the choice was unclear. Each option had relatively equal pros and cons. But Intel was not playing for today's battle. Rather, it was playing with a longer-term objective in mind: to lead the microprocessor industry. In this game, the 8086 battle was less significant, and the right option becomes clear: Intel should license its technology.

Intel submitted to IBM's request. It licensed its 8086 technology to Advanced Micro Devices and other competitors, including IBM. Perhaps because IBM was playing a shorter-term game, the 8086-microprocessor game, IBM welcomed Intel's decision and committed itself to building its PCs around Intel technology. IBM forced Intel's hand and won the 8086 game.

Later, Intel introduced an improved chip, the 286; and a new game began. Intel entered the 286 game with a stronger position—IBM's PCs were built around Intel technology—and so this time it refused to license its technology to competitors. IBM nevertheless adopted the 286. This pattern continued with Intel's subsequent versions, 386, 486, Pentium, Pentium II, and Pentium III.

Because Intel lost the first game and gained IBM's acceptance, it won the stream of subsequent games. It outmaneuvered IBM by thinking one step ahead.

INJURING AN ASSASSIN During the Spring and Autumn period (770–476 B.C.), the emperor of Wu was preoccupied with the prince of Wei. The emperor had taken power by killing the prince's father and assuming the throne. The prince, seeking revenge, was assembling capable men to mount an attack. So the emperor decided to hire an assassin, Yao Li, to get rid of the prince's threat quickly and permanently.

To kill the prince, Yao Li would need to get close. But this would be difficult, because the prince was a careful and suspicious man. He would be wary of anyone who came from within the emperor's domain. So Yao Li proposed a plan to injure himself.

He publicly offended the emperor. In response, the emperor, playing along with the secret plan, ordered Yao Li arrested and his right hand severed in punishment. The one-handed Yao Li fled the emperor. He sought refuge with the prince and swore to now hate the emperor and yearn for revenge.

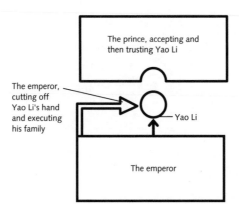

The prince accepted Yao Li into his territory but remained suspicious. He sent spies to investigate the authenticity of Yao Li's falling-out with the emperor. The spies returned with shocking news. Not only had the emperor cut off Yao Li's hand, but he also had Yao Li's wife and children executed and their bodies burned in public. This news softened the prince's suspicions. Yao Li had reason to despise the emperor.

Yao Li eventually became one of the prince's advisors. So when the prince was finally ready to take action, and he launched a water-borne attack on the emperor, Yao Li was on the prince's boat. When their boat reached the middle of the sea, Yao Li turned to the prince and thrust a spear into him. While the prince bled to death, his men subdued Yao Li. But before they reached the shore, Yao Li committed suicide.

By injuring himself, Yao Li earned the prince's trust and made the prince pay dearly for this mistake. Yao Li's tactic differs from Intel's only in that Intel chose to live, while Yao Li passed on the benefits of his sacrifice to his ruler, the emperor.

SUMMARY People are less threatened by the weak. They even trust the weak. So by weakening ourselves, we can gain acceptance for ourselves, our people, or our organizations.

Borrow a Corpse for the Soul's Return

借屍還魂

The powerful is beyond exploitation, but the weak needs help. Exploit and
manipulate the weak for they need you more than you need them.

—FROM *THE 36 STRATAGEMS*

THE PRACTICED DEFINITION of this stratagem differs somewhat
from its original definition. "The powerful" has come to mean the
living. "The weak" has come to mean the dead or the forgotten. So this
stratagem advises that we pick up the dead or forgotten to battle the
living. The tactic of reviving something old, dead, or discarded is called
Borrow a corpse for the soul's return.

Webster's New Universal Unabridged Dictionary defines innovation
as "something new or different introduced." We often collapse the "new"
with the "different" and think that for something to be different it must
be new. But companies achieve advantage through differentiation, not
from newness. Of course, newness has benefits. It can, for example, complicate competitors' efforts to copy our innovation. But it is neither sufficient nor necessary to creating an advantage.

Advantage requires being different. If our adversaries have shed off
old models, ideas, or technology to become "new," we can become different and gain advantage by readopting those discarded models, ideas, or
technology. This is particularly powerful, as we shall see, when our
adversary can no longer return to its old ways.

KEY ELEMENTS:

- You adopt something forgotten/abandoned (a model, idea, or technology)

- Because your adversaries have abandoned it, only you use this thing

- You convert this uniqueness into power

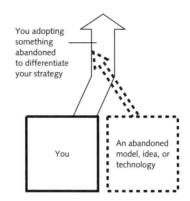

REVIVING THE PAST Southwest Airlines offers a compelling example of the jewels one finds among the discarded. The earliest airlines used a point-to-point model, meaning that you always got a direct flight. They flew, for example, from New York to Chicago, Chicago to Philadelphia, and Philadelphia to New York.

As airline systems grew, this model became unwieldy. Airlines discovered that a hub-and-spoke system was more efficient. This new model helped ensure higher utilization, for example, because it could funnel passengers with the same destination onto one plane even if they embarked from different cities. The result: more consistently full planes.

So airlines established hubs and routed all flights through them.

In the early 1970s, Southwest Airlines shook up the industry by reintroducing the old point-to-point model. Adopting this model was one of

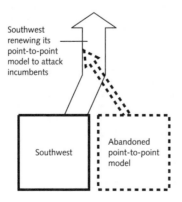

the many choices Southwest made to differentiate its business (Southwest also used one type of airplane rather than multiple and served peanuts instead of meals). But this decision was one of the most difficult for its competitors to copy because they had invested heavily in hubs. As a result, Southwest enjoyed a long period of differentiation.

The story of Southwest's success against significant odds—powerful incumbents, an industry with notoriously poor economics—is now well known. The incumbents tried to copy Southwest's strategy, but they could not break away from their "new" way of doing business. They had moved to a new way of doing business and could not return to the old way. This is what Sun Tzu calls "entangling ground." He writes, "Ground which can be abandoned but is hard to re-occupy is entangling." Ironically, at the core of Southwest's innovation was the decision to return to the past.

THE SHEPHERD CORPSE After the uncle-nephew team of Xiang Liang and Xiang Yu took control of the state of Wu (see Stratagem 23, *Exchange the role of guest for that of host*), they continued their rebellion against the Qin Empire. Their first goal was to reclaim their home state, Chu, whose king had been humiliated and murdered by the Qin.

After they reconquered Chu, and before Xiang Liang was killed during a mission to expand the revolution, Xiang Liang vied for the Chu throne. The former king and his family were dead, so no clear heir existed. Xiang Liang, who came from a long line of respected Chu generals, had as much right to the throne as anyone. Unfortunately for Xiang Liang, a rival warlord claimed he had found a descendant of a noble clan who could be linked, albeit through distant relationships, to the former king. The warlord argued that this person should take the throne.

Xiang Liang consulted a wise man to devise a strategy to maintain control on Chu. This wise man told Xiang Liang to find a direct descendent of the former Chu king. Although he would not directly rule Chu, he could exert influence over the new king. This would also invoke the spirit of the dead Chu king, ignite patriotism, and win Xiang Liang broad support from the Chu people for having discovered a true heir of their beloved former king.

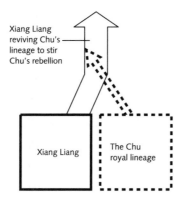

Xiang Liang
reviving Chu's
lineage to stir
Chu's rebellion

Xiang Liang

The Chu
royal lineage

So Xiang Liang launched an exhaustive search. Time and persistence uncovered a direct grandson of the former Chu king—a poor shepherd. The shepherd agreed to become king and adopted his grandfather's name.

The shepherd's coronation marked a pivotal moment for Xiang Liang and the Chu state. It heated fire under the Chu rebellion against the Qin Empire and helped Xiang Liang and his nephew, Xiang Yu, to become leading figures of that rebellion. Had Xiang Liang not found a true descendant to the Chu throne, it is not clear that Chu's patriotic drive would have exploded with sufficient force to put Chu and therefore Xiang Liang at the forefront of rebellion that ended the Qin Empire.

Reviving the history of the Chu king was like borrowing a corpse and using it to awaken Chu's citizens. Southwest and Xiang Liang each revived the past to chart a new future.

SUMMARY As corporations migrate from one model to another, from old technologies to new, they leave behind a valuable trail of sources of innovation—a junkyard of discarded models, ideas, and technology.

These come pretested and, if truly abandoned, can provide a valuable means of differentiation, of creating advantage. Often, competitors who have abandoned models, ideas, and technologies have invested so much in their evolution that they can return only with great effort. In such cases, the junkyard contains true jewels.

PART FOUR

SHANG BING WU BING:
INDIRECT ACTION

上兵無兵

THE EASTERN EQUIVALENT of chess is a strategic board game from China called "go," or sometimes, "I-go." The two games have similar objectives: to remove an opponent's pieces from the board until the winner's pieces dominate or are the only ones standing. But the two approaches to winning are fundamentally different: Chess demands direct attack; go works by indirect attack.

In chess, a person can achieve victory by lining up pieces with one's opponent, then moving the piece directly into the target, knocking it off the board in the process. This is like establishing a line of fire and then pulling the trigger.

Go, on the other hand, takes the opposite approach. The go board markings resemble those of graph paper—a grid of 19 horizontal lines and 19 vertical ones. Go pieces are placed on the intersections of lines, not in the squares as in chess. A total of 361 "spaces" (19 lines × 19 lines) are thus created. Each player begins with a pile of identical stones: One player plays white stones, the other black. Stones are placed on the intersections by turn. The game differs fundamentally from chess in that a player cannot place a piece on an occupied space. Instead, to remove an opponent's pieces from the board, a player must *surround* the opponent's pieces. Once a player has cut off the adversary's freedom of movement, the surrounded piece can be removed.

Chess and go are more than just games. For hundreds of years, they both have been viewed as cultural artifacts and represent a certain historical perspective, because they symbolize our approach to conflict. What they reveal and reinforce is that Western cultures tend toward direct attack while Eastern cultures move indirectly.

INDIRECT WARFARE The preference for indirect action exhibited in go is also evident in Eastern military philosophy. Sun Tzu and the Taoists advocated avoiding direct conflict at almost all costs. They counseled using indirect methods until and unless a situation became too desperate. Sun Tzu wrote, "One skilled at employing the military subdues the other's military but does not do battle,"[i] and "When ten to one, surround them. When five to one, attack them. When two to one, be able to do battle with them."[ii]

In the West, the general rule is if we can beat an adversary, we should attack; if victory is uncertain, we should contain; if victory is unlikely, we should avoid. Both Eastern and Western military approaches contemplate indirect action, but in the West indirect actions are associated with weakness, whereas in the East they are embraced as essential. As Sun Tzu wrote,

> In all fighting, the direct method may be used for joining battle, but indirect methods will be needed in order to secure victory.
>
> Indirect tactics, efficiently applied, are inexhaustible as Heaven and Earth, unending as the flow of rivers and streams; like the sun and moon, they end but to begin anew; like the four seasons, they pass away to return once more.

> In battle, there are not more than two methods of attack—the direct and the indirect; yet these two in combination give rise to an endless series of maneuvers.
>
> The direct and the indirect lead on to each other in turn. It is like moving in a circle—you never come to an end. Who can exhaust the possibilities of their combination? [iii]

In the gap between thought and decision lie invisible rules that guide us Westerners toward the direct path. Our deeply routed metaphors for conflict encourage us toward the direct path and hide from us seemingly circuitous, indirect options. By pausing in this gap and preempting our tendencies, we may reveal winning moves we would otherwise overlook.

Indeed, indirect, competitive moves can deliver significant force using limited energy. They reside in the domain of dominant corporations, not just weak attackers. We can use the stratagems in this section to break out of our conditioned preference for direct approaches; they can trigger our imagination and reveal new options that we might not have thought of before.

Point at the Mulberry
But Curse the Locust

指桑罵槐

When the powerful wants to rule over the weak, he will sound a warning. One's
uncompromising stand will often win loyalty, and one's resolute action, respect.

—FROM *THE 36 STRATAGEMS*

JUST AS PULLING ON one strand of a spider web causes other strands to move, so too do our actions have innumerable unintended consequences. Perhaps because these unintended consequences are so fast, we focus on just a few consequences, usually those intended. Within these unintended, unnoticed consequences lies an opportunity to act invisibly. We can choose actions that send out hidden messages and cause other players in our game to adjust their behavior. As we shall see, corporations use this tactic to lure in "unintended" customers and bring competitors into alignment. Similarly, political leaders have used this to influence new allies and induce them into compliance.

KEY ELEMENTS:

- You want to influence your adversary's behavior

- Rather than attack your adversary directly, you focus your attention on a different target

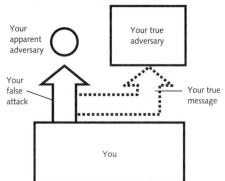

- This action sends a covert message to your adversary which displays your power and communicates your intention

- Your adversary, appreciating your power and intention, alters his behavior

TARGETING ADULTS TO CATCH TEENAGERS In 1999, DreamWorks SKG released *American Beauty*, a film about a father living through a midlife crisis while his family is falling apart. The movie was an unexpected success. Although budgeted as a small niche movie—the studio allotted only $15 million to its production—it earned well over $130 million at the box office.

Somehow this movie expanded far beyond its core audience of 40-something moviegoers. What pushed this low-budget adult film into a mainstream blockbuster? Post-release analysis revealed that young viewers were key. For some reason, Generation Y moviegoers (teenagers) flocked to the film. This is remarkable. For years marketers had been frustrated by the challenge of influencing the highly coveted Generation Y consumer segment. Tactics that had worked on prior generations had no effect on Generation Y consumers. *American Beauty* appeared to have stumbled upon the secret, which might have been that the *American Beauty* message and advertising was never targeted for young viewers in the first place.

So how did *American Beauty,* without even trying, succeed at that which had frustrated marketers for years? Marketers now believe the answer to be that the movie's marketing message, while directed at adults, sent a "hidden" message to teenagers.

This hidden message was that the movie was an authentic adult movie to which teenagers could nonetheless relate. The movie's advertising never appeared to target teenagers directly and so was not something cooked up by marketers to appeal to young viewers. This authenticity appealed to Generation Y teenagers who, marketers have found, do not like being marketed to. In other words, they felt they were choosing to see an adult film, not being told to see something made for their own age group by someone assuming their tastes and culture. At the same time, the movie's advertising gave its teenage characters considerable coverage, thereby giving the teenager audience a sense of a subplot that would speak to their life experiences.

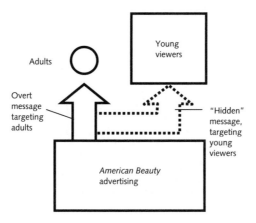

Companies can manipulate consumers and competitors by taking actions that communicates hidden messages. Just as countries use military tests and war games to signal power and ambition, organizations can indirectly influence their adversaries by aiming at one target (e.g., an adult consumer segment), all the while attacking another (in this case, a younger consumer segment).

What makes this tactic possible is the often overlooked interdependency that links industries, companies, and actions. Actions propagate through these connections. This is similar to chaos theory: A butterfly flapping its wings in China may cause rain in Los Angeles; a decision to attack a small competitor has indirect effects, such as influencing the behavior of larger competitors.

By exploring these indirect effects, we may uncover levers of influence, means of achieving goals, that we did not know we had.

ATTACKING A TO INFLUENCE B We can apply the very same tactic used to influence our competitors as was unintentionally applied by the marketers to target *American Beauty* Generation Y consumers.

By attacking one competitor, we can influence the behavior of others to our advantage. For example, to avoid a costly confrontation with a large adversary, we might attack a weak one. Our aggressiveness signals our resolve. Our hidden message might be, "I want this space and will fight over it, so let's stay out of each other's way."

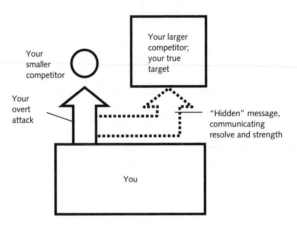

In 1998, British Airways' launch of a new low-fare airline, Go, was viewed by many industry watchers as having a similar intention—to prevent emerging low-fare airlines from challenging British Airways.

A slightly more complex application of this tactic is to pretend to pursue one objective while intending to achieve its opposite. For example, in 1998, Richard Branson, chairman of the Virgin Group, began lobbying the U.S. Congress to repeal the country's foreign ownership restrictions on U.S. airline carriers. His ostensible objective was to open the way for Virgin to acquire a stake in a U.S. carrier larger than the 25 percent maximum allowable by existing law. But industry experts suspected that his true intention was to complicate the aspiration of his archrival British Airways: to establish an alliance with American Airlines. In this case, the hidden message was directed at British Airways and American Airlines. Branson hoped the U.S. Congress would deliver his message to British Airways and American Airlines: "Drop your alliance plans. Virgin will never allow them to succeed."

HUAN UNITES EIGHT STATES In 685 B.C., a new duke, Huan, was installed as ruler of the Qi state. He claimed this position after years of military struggle, and he now wanted to secure peace and build prosperity.

An advisor suggested that the best way to achieve this goal would be to establish an alliance with the eight states in the region, with Duke Huan serving as the leader. The duke thought this would be an excellent plan for peacefully securing power. He invited representatives of the other states to jointly discuss his plan. He built a large platform for the conference; he assured his guests that they would enjoy lavish accommodations; and, as a sign of his peaceful intentions, he did not bring a single war chariot to the meeting.

To the duke's surprise and disappointment, only four of the eight warlords attended his conference. An alliance between just five states would be useless, even counterproductive, because such an alliance could threaten the four states outside the alliance and trigger further conflict. Nevertheless, the five states held the ceremony and appointed Duke Huan leader of their alliance.

At the meeting, Duke Huan proposed that the five new allies attack the four states that did not join the alliance. He requested their support. Three of the four states obliged. However, one, the duke of Song, did not.

The duke of Song was dissatisfied with the results of this meeting. While Song was the largest state, Duke Huan led the alliance. Further, Song saw little value in an alliance that excluded four of the eight states. The duke of Song believed that if he dropped out, others would as well and the alliance would collapse. So during the night, the duke of Song secretly left the meeting.

Song's exit from the alliance infuriated Duke Huan, who ordered a general to hunt down the Duke of Song and kill him. But before his orders could be executed, one of his advisors made an interesting argument. He suggested that Duke Huan let Song alone for the moment. Instead, Duke Huan should focus his attention on a nearby state, one of the four that did not attend the meeting. Such an attack would be safer and cheaper and yet would be an effective warning to Song.

So instead of attacking his primary adversary, the state of Song, Duke Huan attacked a weaker, closer one. He led an army toward the capital city of this weaker, closer state. When he reached the city walls, the head of this small state, fearing a painful defeat, sent an urgent message to Duke Huan explaining that he did not attend the alliance meeting only because he was sick and that he intended to join the alliance. In response, Duke Huan called off his attack, and this smaller state joined the alliance.

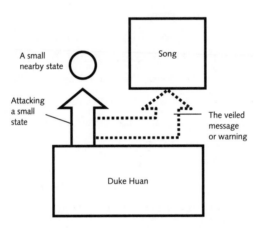

The veiled message in Duke Huan's tactic was powerful. Fearing attack and encouraged by the duke's willingness to forgive old enemies, each state that missed the first meeting apologized and joined the alliance.

This left just Song outside of the alliance. Duke Huan assembled a joint army and marched to Song's capital. But before this army engaged Song, the duke of Song himself, realizing the futility of waging war against seven other states, joined the alliance as well.

Duke Huan unified the eight states, ensuring peace and gaining supreme power without bloodshed. He did this by attacking a weak enemy—pointing at the mulberry while cursing the locust.

SUMMARY Our actions send messages to the other players in our game. Appreciating this, we can choose our actions for the message they send rather than exclusively the direct impact they have. This gives us powerful tools with which to control our game.

Clamor in the East;
Attack to the West

聲東擊西

When the enemy command is in confusion, it will be unprepared for
contingencies. The situation is like flood waters rising higher and higher;
likely to burst the dam at any moment. When the enemy loses
internal control, take the chance and destroy him.

—FROM *THE 36 STRATAGEMS*

DEFENSE IS COMMITMENT: It requires stationing armies, erecting barriers, and consigning assets. By forcing adversaries into defensive postures, we force them into rigidity. Preparedness against one attack makes them vulnerable to another. So by feigning one attack, we increase the effectiveness of another authentic attack.

KEY ELEMENTS:

- You feign an attack

- Your adversary responds to this false attack

- In responding to this attack, your enemy is exposed to your true attack

- You launch your true attack and defeat your adversary

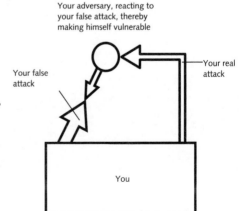

We see this pattern—feign east, attack west—across all realms of competition. On the soccer field, a player pretends to shoot to the left; after the goalie has committed an airborne lunge in that direction, the attacker taps the ball into the right side of the net. In war, an army builds offensive force on one side and then, after the opponent commits troops in defense, attacks an entirely different border. According to retired U.S. Marine Corps brigadier general Samuel B. Griffith II, this tactic can be viewed as the central theme of guerilla warfare:

> Guerilla tactics may be summarized in four Chinese characters pronounced "*Sheng Tung, Chi Hsi*," which mean "Uproar [in the] East; Strike [in the] West." Here we find expressed the all-important principles of distraction on the one hand and concentration on the other; to fix the enemy's attention and to strike where and when he least anticipates the blow.[iv]

This pattern appears less often in business perhaps because it demands a level of secrecy difficult to maintain. But when executed correctly, it can be devastating.

FLICK COLLAPSES FELDMÜHLE NOBEL The Flick Group was a family-owned German conglomerate, headed by Friedrich Karl Flick, who ran the company until 1985, when he transferred ownership to Deutsche Bank. Because he did not anticipate handing control to other family members, he asked Deutsche Bank to realize the greatest value of the company and its substantial equity holdings.

Deutsche Bank consolidated parts of the group into a company called Feldmühle Nobel and sold most of the new company's shares on the open market. The bank retained a 10 percent stake.

Two of Friedrich Karl Flick's nephews were unhappy with Deutsche Bank's handling of the Feldmühle Nobel deal. They believed the bank had failed to get the highest price for the company. To rectify this, they launched a hostile bid for Feldmühle Nobel.

They began accumulating shares in Feldmühle Nobel with the goal of earning enough voting power to force management's hand. But they did not acquire shares by the usual direct method; rather, they bought shares through a series of partners.

The company's board took defensive action. However, because the board expected direct attack, it made a fatal mistake. It passed a resolution restricting any one shareholder's voting rights to 5 percent of the total shares outstanding. This was intended to prevent the Flick brothers from ever having voting power greater than what a 5 percent stake in the company would represent. The Flick brothers would never be able to outvote other shareholders, regardless of the size of their ownership stake.

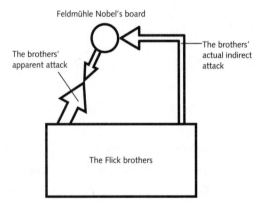

Unfortunately for the company's board, this defense, while effective against a direct attack in which the hostile bidder purchases shares outright, strengthened the Flick brothers' indirect attack. By June 1998, the brothers and their partners had collectively accumulated 36.5 percent of the company. Because these shares were held in three different sets instead of just one, they represented three sets of 5 percent voting rights. A third company who had similarly wanted to take over Feldmühle Nobel but chose a direct approach had accumulated a large chunk of stock worth only 5 percent of voting rights. To win control of the company, this third company had to buy out the Flick brothers' stake at a significant premium. Thus, the Flick brothers realized the higher value they felt their father's company deserved.

By attempting to defend itself against a direct attack, the company's board exposed themselves to an indirect attack. The brothers took advantage of this weakness and achieved their goal.

> *Attack him where he is unprepared.*
> *Appear where not expected.*
>
> —SUN TZU, *THE ART OF WAR*[v]

CROSSING A RIVER, LURING A LEADER, ENDING A SIEGE Two rival warlords, Yuan Shao and the great strategist Cao Cao, had been at war for many years. In A.D. 200, they prepared for what would be their decisive battle. Yuan Shao enjoyed two advantages in this battle. He occupied a superior position, and his forces outnumbered Cao Cao's.

Emboldened by his strength, Yuan Shao decided to cut off Cao Cao's supply lines, support, and escape route by attacking a small city called Baima at the rear of Cao Cao's forces (see Stratagem 10, *Remove the firewood from under the pot*). He ordered enough soldiers to move against Baima so that Cao Cao's forces there would be overwhelmed.

When Cao Cao heard of Yuan Shao's troop movement, he quickly assembled his advisors. They pondered his options but found few to choose from. If they moved to defend Baima, they would be far outnumbered and probably lose that battle. If they did not defend Baima, they would become crippled without supplies and support. They would have no chance against Yuan Shao.

Then one advisor suggested that Cao Cao pretend to attack Yuan Shao's old stronghold, Ye. Cao Cao understood how this move would play out and agreed.

Cao Cao led troops across the river toward Ye. When Yuan Shao heard of this incursion, he ordered half of his forces to turn back from their march toward Baima to return and defend against the imminent attack of Ye. After night set in, however, Cao Cao ordered his troops to change direction. They marched all night toward Baima.

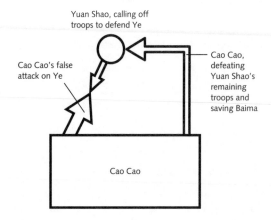

The next morning, Yuan Shao arrived at Ye confused. He was prepared for battle but found no enemy. No one at Ye even knew an attack was coming.

That same morning, Cao Cao arrived at Baima with the troops he had redirected. His army now outnumbered the half that Yuan Shao had left to besiege Baima. He defeated Yuan Shao's forces, cut off their general's head, and saved the city.

SUMMARY Cao Cao and the Flick brothers each tricked their adversaries into impossible situations. They each feigned an attack, the defense against which forced their adversaries to expose themselves to a second attack. By then launching this second attack, the Flick brothers realized the high value they thought their family's company was worth and Cao Cao saved a strategically important city from attack.

Appearance and intention inevitably ensnare people when artfully used,
even if people sense that there is an ulterior intention behind the overt

appearance. When you set up your ploys and opponents fall for them, then you win by letting them act on your ruse.

As for those who do not fall for a ploy, when you see they will not fall into one trap, you have another one set. Then, even if opponents have not fallen for your original ploy, in effect they actually have.

—YAGYU MUNENORI, *THE BOOK OF FAMILY TRADITIONS ON THE ART OF WAR*[vi]

Openly Repair the Walkway, Secretly March to Chen Cang

暗渡陳倉

To pin down the enemy, expose part of your action deliberately,
so that you can make a surprise attack somewhere else.

—FROM *THE 36 STRATAGEMS*

WHILE THEIR ADVERSARIES fix their attention on the orthodox path, the more creative companies and armies travel along the unorthodox path. Hannibal did this when he crossed the Alps with elephants to steal the advantage and catch his Roman adversaries off guard.

KEY ELEMENTS:

- You focus your adversary, or let your adversary focus, on a direct orthodox attack

- You launch an indirect unorthodox attack

- This indirect unorthodox action surprises your adversary

- You take the advantage

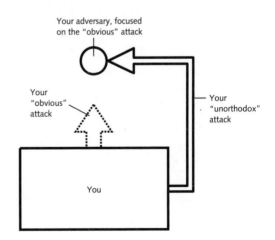

BUILDING DOMINANCE FROM UNORTHODOXY Hindustan-Lever performed an unorthodox maneuver, which has challenged the competition for decades. Through creative marketing and distribution tactics, this company increased its revenue by 25 percent annually during the ten-year period from 1991 to 2000 to become the leading provider of soap, shampoo, and other personal care products in India. The company owes much of its success to shunning the traditional path taken by even its parent company, Unilever, and opting for untraditional methods to reach Indian consumers.

Hindustan-Lever's strategic innovation is driven by two characteristics that differentiate Indian consumers from Unilever's European and North American customers. First, Indian consumers are poor. Sixty percent live below the poverty line. Second, these disadvantaged buyers live in rural areas and are therefore difficult to reach. Yet these rural consumers cannot be ignored. At 500 million people, they represent a population that is 70 percent larger than that of the United States.

So how does Hindustan-Lever overcome the obvious barriers of trying to reach seemingly unreachable consumers, especially when its competition has tripped time and again when trying to reach Indian consumers? How does it deal with the lack of proper roads and communication when very few of these consumers have televisions? How does it sell soap to patrons who lack education and for whom daily washing is not a regular habit? Hindustan-Lever does it by choosing paths its adversaries overlook.

Unilever, and its consumer product peers, depend heavily on television to build brand and product awareness. But what do you do when no televisions exist, as is the case in rural India? The orthodox approach is to focus efforts on consumers with televisions—the middle-class urban Indian. This is the path most consumer goods companies in India have chosen. Hindustan-Lever, however, took the indirect approach. Because television was not a viable means through which to distribute commercials, the company reasoned: Why not distribute advertising through another medium? The company worked with Ogilvy Outreach, a division of Ogilvy & Mather, to produce a series of traveling theater shows. They hired entertainers, including dancers, actors, and magicians, assembled them into fifty teams, prepared localized scripts, and put the shows on the road.

At each town, a show unfolds that is part entertainment and part commercial. The play's plot might infuse lessons about hygiene, a low-tech version of product placement, while backdrops featuring images of Unilever soap products serve the function of commercials. The result is television delivered via a physical rather than electromagnetic channel.

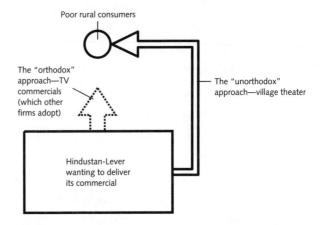

Hindustan-Lever's other marketing innovations follow a similar pattern: taking an unorthodox, seemingly less direct approach while its competitors focus on the orthodox one. For example, rural consumers wash less and consequently use less soap. Hindustan-Lever's competitors noted and accepted this as another reason to concentrate on urban markets. Hindustan-Lever reacted differently by aiming to educate rural consumers as to the importance of more regular washing. For example, they set up a marketing team at a local festival. The team used an infrared light to show festival-goers that invisible germs had actually collected on their hands, even though they looked clean. Through such education efforts, Hindustan-Lever was able to build per capita soap consumption and thus a market for itself. The process required two steps—education and then sale—rather than the one-step process that competitors used. By using these highly imaginative methods, however, Hindustan-Lever established a competitive advantage, in the form of superior brand awareness with the rural poor.

THE CIRCUITOUS MARCH EASTWARD In 207 B.C., the Qin dynasty was in rebellion. Two rival rebel leaders struggled for control of Guangzhong, a strategically important kingdom of the Qin dynasty. One rebel leader, Liu Bang, had originally conquered the kingdom. But another stronger rebel leader, Xiang Yu, wanted the territory as well. Because Xiang Yu's forces outnumbered Liu Bang's, Liu Bang was forced to concede the kingdom.

Despite his capitulation, Xiang Yu remained wary of Liu Bang's ambitions. So he devised a plan to keep Liu Bang as far away from Guangzhong as possible. He divided the kingdom into eighteen parts and appointed Liu Bang as the leader of a remote area at the west end of the kingdom. To further insulate himself against Liu Bang's potential threat, he divided the area between the capital and Liu Bang's fiefdom into three parts and appointed three generals as leaders of each of these. One of the fiefdoms was called Cheng Cang.

Liu Bang was already upset at having to give up the kingdom he initially conquered. He was now even angrier for being banished to a far corner of the region. As he and his soldiers marched out of Guangzhong's capital, one of his advisors suggested that they destroy the wooden road that connected their new home in the west with the capital. This would put Xiang Yu at rest by assuring him that Liu Bang had no intention of returning eastward to seek revenge. Liu Bang agreed, and so his soldiers destroyed roads and bridges as they traveled.

Once he established his new base, Liu Bang ordered his general to rebuild the army. When the army was so strong that Liu Bang felt it could defeat Xiang Yu's, he summoned his general. They discussed how best to march eastward and retake the kingdom. Two barriers stood in their way. First, three generals ruled the territory surrounding their new fiefdom that lay between them and the capital. Second, the wooden road that led to Xiang Yu was in ruins. However, Liu Bang and his general were wise men. They crafted a clever strategy to overcome, even draw strength from, these barriers.

Liu Bang ordered a contingent of men who set about rebuilding the wooden walkway. This impacted Liu Bang's adversaries in two ways. First, it put them off guard. Liu Bang's workforce was so small that it would take years for them to complete the job—or so his adversaries thought. Second, his plan focused his enemies on the "obvious" path. Both Xiang Yu and the general of neighboring Cheng Cang saw that if Liu Bang ever did rebuild the walkway, they could easily block his attack by concentrating their forces at the mouth of the narrow passage.

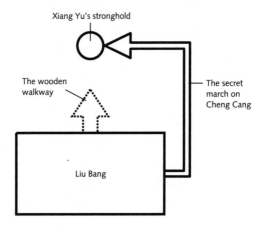

But Liu Bang had no intention of using his walkway. His construction project was merely a diversion. He planned to attack Xiang Yu by another, unorthodox route.

While his opposition watched the walkway, Liu Bang ordered his troops to attack Cheng Cang, his neighboring state. He surprised Cheng Cang's general and took the fiefdom. This move caught his adversaries off guard and broadened Liu Bang's base of power. It laid the foundation for a campaign in which Liu Bang sequentially expanded his growing power base, defeating the states standing between him and Guangzhong's capital, until he reached Xiang Yu. Liu Bang ultimately won back control of Guangzhong, took command of the rebel movement, unified China, and became the founding emperor of the Han Empire.

SUMMARY Hindustan-Lever and Liu Bang each focused their adversaries on the obvious, orthodox path. They each capitalized on the opportunity their adversaries thereby presented, each choosing the unorthodox path, taking their adversaries by surprise, and seizing victory.

Fool the Emperor and Cross the Sea

瞞天過海

The perception of perfect preparation leads to relaxed vigilance.
Familiar sights lead to slackened suspicion. Therefore, secret machinations
are better concealed in the open than in the dark, and extreme
public exposure often contains extreme secrecy.

—FROM *THE 36 STRATAGEMS*

EVERY ENVIRONMENT (e.g., market, sector, and industry) has background noise composed of everyday actions that attract no particular attention. Each day, for instance, realtors buy real estate, producers build factories, investors buy shares. As we grow accustomed to these familiar occurrences, they become background noise.

This background noise offers an opportunity, however, because in it, we can hide our actions. We can weave a façade of normalcy around our adversaries and within, not behind the façade, we can execute our strategy. The tactic Disney used to acquire its land—hiding its actions in the open among everyday actions—is what *The 36 Stratagems* calls *Fool the emperor and cross the sea.*

KEY ELEMENTS:

- Your adversary is vigilant
- You take actions that appear normal (e.g., that

appear to be everyday actions)

- Your adversary fixes his attention on this façade of normalcy. He does not see your true attack or intention

- You take your adversary

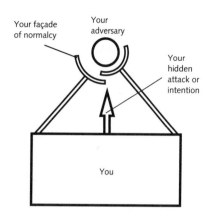

This stratagem originates from the story of an emperor who refused to cross the sea despite his general's urging. The general ordered his soldiers to build large barges on the water and decorate them with dirt, trees, and military tents so that they appeared to be a normal encampment on solid ground. He then invited the emperor to enter the camp. As the emperor sat comfortably entertained inside a windowless tent, the barges were launched and navigated to another shore. The general fooled the emperor and crossed the sea.[vii] The core lesson here is that by making actions appear normal, we hide our attack in the open and we still do not provoke a response from our adversary.

HIDING ACTION AMONG "NORMAL PRACTICES" Industries tend to focus on a common set of variables to monitor competition. The television industry focuses on ratings; the pharmaceutical industry, on new patents; and investors, on transactions. If you are particularly careful not to disturb these variables, you can hide your actions in them. This is moving under the cover of stillness.

As an example, consider Krupp AG's 1991 acquisition of Hoesch AG in Germany. Throughout the 1980s, Krupp courted Hoesch with proposals of friendly mergers, all of which were rejected. Krupp nevertheless believed that a merger would be beneficial, perhaps even necessary, so it chose to pursue a more aggressive tactic. It decided to attempt to take Hoesch over by buying a controlling interest in the company.

Krupp knew, however, that Hoesch could easily mount an effective defense if it became aware of Krupp's intentions. It knew that industry players would look for evidence of such takeover intentions in financial

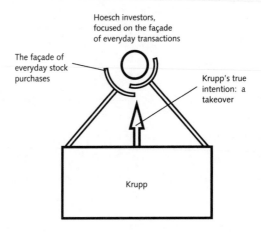

transactions, such as unusually concentrated purchases of Hoesch's stock. Krupp, therefore, had to find a way to hide its stock purchases and fend off a defensive response by Hoesch.

Both Krupp and Hoesch are German firms, and as such, practiced the "house bank" tradition whereby a company maintains close ties with its primary bank. Typically, a German company's house bank is a significant shareholder in the company, sits on the company board, and is involved in upper-level management. In order to hide its actions, Krupp would have to deviate from this tradition. It did not inform its house bank, or any of its major banks, of the actions it was about to take.

Over the course of six months, Krupp slowly and anonymously purchased Hoesch shares through a Swiss bank. Because the stock purchases appeared to be "normal" everyday transactions, Krupp was able to collect 24.9 percent of Hoesch without triggering suspicion. By the time Krupp announced its holdings in October 1991, it was too late for Hoesch to defend itself effectively or for competitors to provoke a bidding war.

Krupp successfully gained control of Hoesch by hiding its unusual actions behind a veil of normalcy.

The Walt Disney Company employed the same tactic when it purchased land for Disney World in the 1960s. Had landowners discovered that Disney was purchasing 30,000 acres of land in Florida, land prices would have risen quickly. By assembling the land from pieces purchased anonymously, Disney effectively hid its intentions and avoided paying premiums.

CAPACITY AS A WEAPON Making decisions to build or close factories is an everyday part of business. Companies regularly make such decisions in order to optimize production efficiency. If a company has too much capacity, it must close plants to stave off losses on unused buildings and land. If a company has too little capacity, it must build new factories in order to prevent competitors from capturing market share and to ensure that it runs machines efficiently.

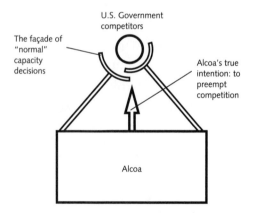

Companies, however, can also use production capacity to influence their competitors. Building capacity influences your competitors' business plans and therefore their behavior. The Aluminum Company of America (Alcoa) appreciated the powerful influence that seemingly "normal" capacity decisions can have on their competitors. After many years, the U.S. government saw the true intention behind these so-called normal decisions too.

In 1945, Alcoa was convicted of using capacity to unfairly dominate its competition. The plaintiff in the case argued that Alcoa regularly built more capacity than projected demand warranted. By doing so, Alcoa signaled to its competition that it would fight aggression with heavy price cuts. To understand this, consider Alcoa's position once it sunk money into a new factory. If a competitor attempted to steal market share from this factory, it would make economic sense for Alcoa to cut prices until they equaled its direct product cost, even if this resulted in overall losses. In capital-intensive businesses such as Alcoa's, this price level results in considerable losses. Alcoa, in effect, precommitted itself to enter a price war if competition entered that could make both itself and its competition unprofitable. Understanding this, a competitor would not challenge Alcoa, because to do so would be suicide. Although Alcoa appeared to behave in a normal fashion, the courts ruled that its actions were anticompetitive.

LULLING AN OPPONENT WITH REPETITION In the late 500s, the founder of the Sui dynasty defeated the northern kingdoms and decided to expand his successful military campaign south of the Yangtze River. He assigned a general named He Nuobi to lead his first southern effort: a siege of the Chen kingdom just across the Yangtze.

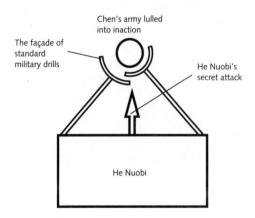

He Nuobi assembled an army and set up camp on the river's edge just opposite Chen's northern border. The Chen king ordered his troops to set up positions on the other shore in preparation for the attack. Both armies were poised for battle.

Soon, He Nuobi ordered his army to prepare for battle. At the sounds of the activity, the Chen army took their positions and prepared for an attack. The Sui army marched, drums beat, and dust rose into the air, but no attack came.

The Sui army was conducting maneuvers. These continued for several days. Eventually the Chen army grew weary of maintaining their vigilance. They grew accustomed to the sounds of war and stopped associating them with an attack.

He Nuobi had purchased boats and hidden them for just this moment. One evening, once he was sure he could move his troops without triggering a reaction from the Chen army, he quietly crossed the river. He and his soldiers reached shore at dawn and surprised the Chen forces. They easily defeated the Chen and established a foothold south of the Yangtze.

SUMMARY He Nuobi, Disney, Alcoa, and Krupp each outmaneuvered their opponent by hiding their actions within a façade of everyday occurrences. These occurrences incited no concern. Indeed, in each instance, they lulled the adversaries into inaction. By the time the adversaries realized they were being attacked, selling out, being acquired, or otherwise giving up power, it was too late.

> *The general who is skilled in defense hides in the most secret recesses of the earth; he who is skilled in attack flashes forth from the topmost heights of heaven.*
>
> —SUN TZU, *THE ART OF WAR*[viii]

Create Something
Out of Nothing

無中生有

Design a counterfeit front to put the enemy off guard.
When the trick works, the front is changed into something real so that
the enemy will be thrown into a state of double confusion. In short,
deceptive appearances often conceal forthcoming danger.

—FROM *THE 36 STRATAGEMS*

WHEN WE PLAY most simple games, like chess or football, we are limited to a fixed number of pieces and players. We cannot add new pieces to the board. In go, we can add players but not move them. But real-world games, such as business, war, and politics offer more freedom because we can add pieces and players in addition to moving them.

"Real world" games are not closed systems; however, we often overlook this fact. We tend to play business as we play chess or football. We do not usually think about adding new players to the board. This is why companies that break this unspoken rule surprise their competitors. While their competitors are thinking about what to do with the players on the field, creative companies introduce a brand-new player and change the game. *The 36 Stratagems* calls the tactic of adding a new player to the game *Create something out of nothing*.

KEY ELEMENTS:

- Your direct attack (i.e., one using existing players) is ineffective

- You create a new player/entity

- This player/entity catches your adversary off guard

- You or the new player/entity take your adversary

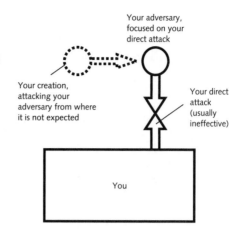

Things in the world arise of Existence, and Existence arises from Nonexistence.

—LAO TZU, *TAO TE CHING*

COKE CREATES THE BOTTLER OF ITS DREAMS In the early 1980s, the Coca-Cola Company was struggling against its historical archrival Pepsi. Its flagship product, Coca-Cola, was losing share relative to Pepsi-Cola. By 1985, for the first time in history, Pepsi-Cola commanded a larger share of the U.S. soft drink market than Coca-Cola.

One of Coca-Cola's challenges was that Pepsi's distribution model was different and, for a key customer segment, superior. Pepsi used a centralized bottling system that served large regional grocery chains better that Coca-Cola's web of small local bottlers.

At first glance, it appeared that Coca-Cola had two options. It could convince its independent bottlers to merge, or it could take them over.

The first option would be excessively expensive. So Coca-Cola attempted the second. It began buying up poorly managed bottlers and selling them to better managed bottlers with the hope of triggering the creation of larger regional bottling companies.

Coca-Cola pursued this tactic for years but could not stem its market share decline. The regional bottlers whose development Coca-Cola encouraged were not large or numerous enough to have a sufficient impact. The company needed to find a more potent tactic. Playing the existing pieces on Coca-Cola's game board offered no attractive options. So, Coca-Cola decided to change the game by adding a new player to the board.

In 1986, Coca-Cola created an independent bottling subsidiary, Coca-Cola Enterprises (CCE). This became Coca-Cola's first large regional, "anchor" bottler. CCE was not an extension of Coca-Cola. It was a brand new independent company. Fifty-one percent of its shares were sold to the public.

CCE purchased a string of bottlers and consolidated them into a regional network. This enabled it to compete effectively with Pepsi for regional grocery chain customers. CCE also achieved significant cost

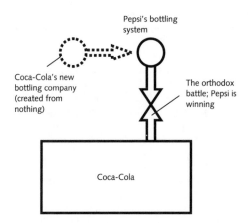

savings by renegotiating superior terms with suppliers and retailers, merging purchasing where possible, and cutting its workforce by 20 percent.

By creating something from nothing, Coca-Cola helped reverse the trend of its eroding market share and regained dominance of the cola market.

The tactic was so successful that Pepsi copied it twelve years later. In 1998, Pepsi creating a separate bottling operation company called the Pepsi Bottling Group (PBG). By the end of the year, PBG handled 32 percent of Pepsi's worldwide volume.

CREATING CUSTOMERS A common application of this tactic of creating something out of nothing is to create your own customer. After World War I, for example, Boeing was struggling to fill its high wartime capacity. The U.S. Postal Service was about to award a contract to deliver its airmail. Boeing wanted to make sure that whoever won that contract bought its planes from Boeing and not from its rival, Douglas. So Boeing decided to add a new player to the game, one that would be completely loyal to Boeing. It created an airline that later became United Airlines. When United won the U.S. Postal Service's contract, it purchased planes from Boeing. In this way the company outmaneuvered Douglas.

GUERILLAS In 1937, Mao Tse-tung put down on paper his principles of guerilla warfare in an influential book titled *On Guerilla Warfare*. The principles outlined in his book proved powerful. By following them, his movement systematically captured land and power from the Chinese Nationalist government led by Chiang Kai-shek. Over the course of twelve years, the Communists routed the government and took control of the country.

Mao Tse-tung's guerilla tactics were successful in part because they added new players to the game while his more orthodox and structured opponent maneuvered players already in the game.

When Mao Tse-tung's rebels set their targets on a new town, before taking up arms they launched a recruitment effort. Rebel teams walked the countryside to recruit, convert, and train local residents. These residents, in turn, recruited other residents, until eventually the rebels could count on an organized group of supporters.

Later, when the rebel forces launched their actual attack, they did so with a key advantage: a base of support to provide information and supplies. The town's leadership found itself battling an enemy it never expected. Its own citizens undermined the city's defense. In effect, Mao Tse-tung's rebels added a new opponent to the game before they engaged in battle.

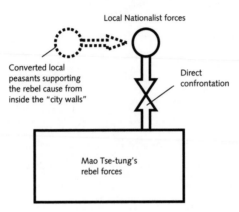

Mao Tse-tung flustered his opponents, appearing in unexpected places. Using this principle, he was able to circumvent enemy lines by creating rebels behind them while attacking them. He repeated this pattern—recruit, build support, attack from inside and out—consistently and methodically until he routed the Nationalist government and seized control of the nation.

SUMMARY Our adversaries expect us to play with the pieces already on the board. They rarely contemplate us introducing new pieces; so when we do, we take our adversary off-guard. Coca-Cola introduced a new bottler to attack Pepsi. Mao Tse-tung introduced a new enemy inside his enemy's town. Both surprised and outmaneuvered their targets.

Hide a Dagger Behind a Smile

笑裏藏刀

*One way or another, make the enemies trust you and thereby slacken
their vigilance. Meanwhile, plot secretly, making preparations for
your future action to ensure its success.*

—FROM *THE 36 STRATAGEMS*

A THREATENED ADVERSARY will resist; a trusting one will not. This is why highly competitive companies often go out of their way to maintain "friendly" appearances. They take what seem labored circuitous routes to avoid triggering resistance in their adversaries. *The 36 Stratagems* terms this tactic *Hide a dagger behind a smile.*

KEY ELEMENTS:

- A direct attack would generate resistance in your adversary

- You choose an approach that is, or appears to be, friendly

- Your adversary lets down defenses and welcomes this approach

- You take your adversary with a secondary or hidden attack

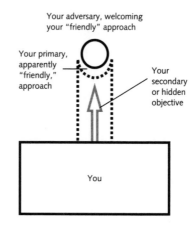

Your adversary, welcoming your "friendly" approach

Your primary, apparently "friendly," approach

Your secondary or hidden objective

You

The key goal of this stratagem is to convince your adversaries to put down their guards. In business, companies usually achieve this by taking actions that are genuinely pleasant. In war, this is usually achieved by taking actions that only appear placating but actually hide unfriendly intentions.

INTEL SMILES AND TAKES CONSUMERS Adopting friendly appearances does not need to be deceitful. Intel, for example, genuinely helped computer manufacturers with a problem that they jointly shared: Consumers were not upgrading their computers by buying new ones. In convincing consumers to upgrade (the primary objective), Intel achieved a second objective that did not benefit computer manufacturers. It gained new power and profits at the cost of the manufacturers it was out to help.

In the early 1990s, computer manufacturers' sales targets were at risk because consumers were not upgrading. They were satisfied with their old computers, built on Intel's slower 286 chips, but had little urge to buy new computers, built on Intel's 386 chips. So, in 1989, Intel decided to take action.

Intel crafted a new marketing campaign that diverged dramatically from what it, and component makers like it, had undertaken before. Traditionally, component manufacturers market their products to the equipment manufacturers using their products. They do not market directly to consumers, because consumers do not decide what components to buy—they decide what machine to buy. For example, consumers do not choose which motor they want in their refrigerators; they just choose refrigerators. So motor manufacturers do not waste money marketing to consumers. Rather, they market to refrigerator manufacturers.

Intel decided to challenge this traditional approach. It launched the now famous "Intel Inside" campaign, directly targeting consumers, in order to stimulate consumer upgrades. As Dennis Carter, the marketer behind Intel's consumer marketing drive, said, "Our product was becoming more important in defining the personal computer and what it could do. But the general public was not keeping up with changes in technology. I believed we needed to start talking with the end users."[ix] Intel placed the "Intel Inside" logo on almost all computers using Intel's chips and on all print advertising, point-of-sale merchandising, shipping cartons, and packaging.

The campaign had two impacts. The primary impact was that consumers became more aware of the technology inside computers and therefore found a new reason to upgrade their computers. As Michael Dell, the founder, president, and CEO of Dell, said, "With just two words—Intel Inside—Dennis [Carter] has been able to simplify the complexity of microelectronics and create a level of comfort in our technology for millions of personal computer buyers."[x] Computer manufacturers naturally cheered the results.

The secondary impact of Intel's campaign was less obvious. Had it not been linked to spurring new computer sales, Intel might not have received the level of cooperation from computer manufacturers that it

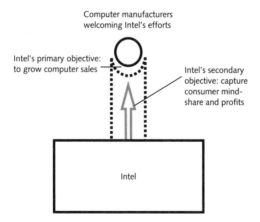

did. The campaign gave Intel more power over consumers. It now controlled a new "switch" for triggering consumer upgrades—processor speed—and therefore could decide when manufacturers would introduce a new line of computers.

It also now wielded a consumer brand, which gave, and still gives, Intel greater bargaining power with computer manufacturers and a larger share of profits from each computer.

Because Intel's consumer marketing campaign spurred computer upgrades, computer manufacturers supported it. But through the campaign, Intel secured a secondary benefit, one that computer manufacturers would not have supported on its own: Intel took consumer mindshare and profits from computer manufacturers.

THE JAPANESE BECOME AMERICAN To stave off the unexpected success of Japanese cars in the United States, the big three U.S. car manufacturers appealed to consumers' national pride. They launched a "Buy American" campaign.

Japanese manufacturers needed to devise a strategy for countering this campaign, for deflating the resistance to Japanese cars that was building among U.S. consumers. The obvious responses—increasing marketing spending, launching a counter-campaign—might further agitate consumers.

So instead of attacking the "Buy American" campaign directly, Japanese car manufacturers simply became more American. They opened manufacturing plants in the United States, and increased the number of American jobs supported by their car sales. So when GM advised a consumer to Buy American, that consumer would consider buying a Toyota Corolla. Japanese car manufacturers pacified their adversaries' resistance by becoming friendly.

AN OLD FRIEND'S SMILE In 342 B.C., the states of Qin and Wei were at war. The king of Wei was worried. His army had recently lost a battle and was weak and of low morale. His army was in no condition to engage the 50,000 Qin soldiers marching toward one of Wei's cities. The king wanted to avoid battle, so he assembled his advisors to study his options.

One of his ministers offered a bloodless plan. As a boy, he had known the Qin general who was now in charge of the approaching army. He believed he could appeal to this friendship and persuade the general to call off his siege. The king of Wei approved this plan and charged this minister with defending the threatened Wei city. The minister rushed off to take his position in the city waiting for the approach of the Qin army.

When the Qin general arrived with his troops, he learned that his old boyhood friend, the minister, was in charge of the city's defenses and that he wanted a meeting to negotiate peace. The general chose his response carefully. He was not interested in peace, but he did not want to reveal this. As long as the city believed that peace was an option, their defenses would remain loose. If they felt that an attack was imminent, they would hole themselves up behind well-fortified walls, making the siege more costly. So the Qin general warmly welcomed his old friend's proposal.

Three days later, the two friends met at a designated location. To prove his good intentions, the Wei minister brought only 300 soldiers with him. The Qin general, to display his warm intentions, invited the entire Wei party to a banquet.

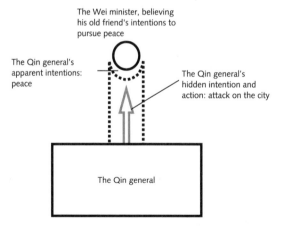

At the banquet, the Qin general and the Wei minister drank and ate together as one would expect of boyhood friends. But before the banquet ended, Qin soldiers kidnapped the Wei minister and his soldiers. They stole their captives' uniforms and marched toward the city disguised as

Wei soldiers. When they arrived, the city's guards opened the city gates, believing them to be the Wei minister and his party returning from their negotiations. The Qin soldiers rushed in and took control over the unsuspecting city.

By appearing pleasant, the Qin general was able to keep his adversary off guard. He moved into the opening that this tactic created to quickly, efficiently, and nearly bloodlessly defeat his adversary.

SUMMARY The Qin general, Intel, and Japanese car manufacturers each benefited from launching attacks welcomed by their adversaries. Because their attacks appeared friendly, their adversaries offered no resistance.

Deck the Tree with Bogus Blossoms

樹上開花

Use deceptive appearances to make your troop formation look more powerful than it is. When wild geese soar high above, the grandness of their formation is greatly enhanced by the display of their outstretched wings.

—FROM *THE 36 STRATAGEMS*

To SUCCEED AGAINST a stronger competitor, creative companies coordinate with their environments to build power. They form networks of alliances that together are stronger than their parts. A bee is a bother, but a swarm can be dangerous. A buffalo is no match for a lion, but a herd is safe. *The 36 Stratagems* terms this tactic *Deck the tree with bogus blossoms.*

KEY ELEMENTS:

- You are too weak to attack your adversary alone

- You coordinate individual elements within your organization or in your environment

- Coordinated, these parts become a much stronger whole

- You are now strong enough to defeat your adversary

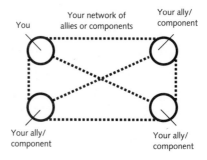

ALLIANCES VS. OWNERSHIP In the early 1980s, Ford, Chrysler, and General Motors (GM) were fighting off car imports from Japan and Europe. Success would depend significantly on improving quality. So they took on this challenge.

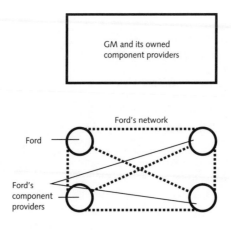

Although Ford and Chrysler were much smaller than GM, they improved their quality more rapidly during the 1980s and early 1990s. Unlike GM, with its vertically integrated infrastructure, Ford and Chrysler did not own the manufacturers that supplied switches, motors, and other car components. The network of independent component manufacturers approximated the strength of GM's proprietary network, but was more flexible. Ford and Chrysler could, for example, more easily switch providers and force them to improve quality. GM had to fund its own upgrades directly and was more resistant to switching manufacturing plants, because it owned the plants themselves.

FIGHTING GOLIATH Microsoft's competitors are adopting a similar approach—creating a network of alliances—to contain their powerful adversary. In 2001, for example, Sun, American Express, GM, United Airlines, and other companies formed an organization called the Liberty Alliance. The Liberty Alliance's aim is to develop a standard that allows users to log on to the Internet one time, through multiple devices, and use its profiles on a range of online services.[xi] While they do not explicitly state that their objective is to fight Microsoft, their objective is clearly a response to Microsoft's efforts to develop a similar standard. If Microsoft develops this standard, it will be able to hold other players hostage and extract profits as it has done with DOS and Windows. The Liberty Alliance wants to prevent this by establishing its standard first. Sun's representative to the group asked other members at a meeting in 2002, "Would any of you be here if it wasn't for Microsoft?"[xii]

Similarly, in 1998, a group of handset makers that included Nokia, Ericsson, and Motorola teamed up to create a new company, Symbian. Over the years, they had seen what Microsoft did to IBM—take control of a key lucrative component (the operating system)—and did not want their handsets to suffer the same fate. If Microsoft were to dominate the

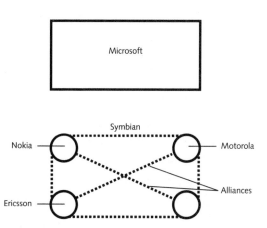

cell-phone operating system market as it does the market for computer operating systems, handsets would become commodities with little more margin than personal computer clones. Individually, none of the companies in the Symbian alliance have the cash or software competency to compete with Microsoft. But by coordinating their efforts, they hope to create a viable adversary for Microsoft.

By coordinating individual parts in their environments, such as creating a network of alliances, creative companies are able to approximate the power of much larger adversaries. They transform themselves from bees to a swarm; from one buffalo to a herd of buffalos.

Ironically, Microsoft pursues the same tactic but uses company-owned assets rather than adversaries in a coalition. As described earlier, the company coordinates its products so that they support each other. By bundling its software products and ensuring that they are compatible with each other, Microsoft creates a more valuable network of products.

BULL WARRIORS During the Warring States period (475–221 B.C.), five states joined forces against Qi. Unable to resist such uneven odds, Qi lost more than seventy cities during the course of five years, until only two cities remained. Both of those cities were surrounded. One was under the command of the capable general, Tian Dan.

Tian Dan knew that he was outnumbered and could not defeat his attackers with orthodox methods. Without a brilliant plan, he would remain trapped until his people either surrendered or died of hunger. So he analyzed his nonmilitary assets and wondered how he could coordinate these into becoming powerful enough to break his enemy's encirclement.

His audit identified two useful nonmilitary assets: he had people—women, children, and elderly—who were not slated for military duty, and he possessed more than a thousand bulls.

Tian Dan issued three directives. First, he ordered these women, children, and elderly to guard the city walls and to enroll in the military. Second, he had the bulls outfitted for battle. He ordered them covered with silk sheets painted in colorful patterns with knives fastened to their horns and oil-soaked straw bundles tied to their tails. Third, he collected gold from the citizens. Then he asked a group of wealthy men to bring the money to his enemy's general. They delivered the message that the city was about to fall and the general was requested not to take their wives and children. This third order put his enemy off guard. The enemy soldiers celebrated their pending return home, and then they slept soundly.

That night, however, after his enemy's soldiers had fallen asleep, Tian Dan executed his plan. He had the oil-soaked straw bundles that were tied to the bulls' tails lit, and then released the bulls outside the city walls, where they ran wild. The enemy soldiers woke up to find themselves

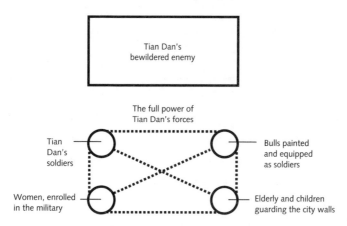

under attack by strange ferocious beasts. Many fled for their lives. Tian Dan then ordered his soldiers to march on the enemy forces. They could do this in greater numbers, because women fought with them as the elderly citizens and children guarded the city walls.

Tian Dan's bewildered enemy fell. His city was saved. This triumph marked the beginning of a series of victories for Qi that led to the state recovering the cities that had been lost, returning Qi to its former splendor.

SUMMARY By coordinating the elements around him, Tian Dan approximated much greater power than each element could have exerted alone. Similarly, by coordinating their efforts, Microsoft's adversaries hope to pose a sufficiently significant threat to hold back a seemingly unstoppable adversary. A buffalo holds little chance against a lion, but in a herd it is safe.

To Catch the Bandits,
First Capture Their Leader

擒賊擒王

*Capture their chief, and the enemy will collapse. His situation will be
as desperate as a sea dragon fighting on land.*

—FROM *THE 36 STRATAGEMS*

CREATIVE AND COMPETITIVE companies pull levers that other
companies do not think of. For example, to influence a competitor,
they often save energy by going directly to their competitor's leadership,
which is similar to leading a horse by directing its head. *The 36 Stratagems* terms this tactic *To catch the bandits, first capture their leader.*

KEY ELEMENTS:

- You face a persistent
  adversary

- You identify your adversary's leader or leaders

- You aim your attack at
  this leader or these leaders

- Your adversary's leadership falls and brings
  down your adversary's
  organization with it

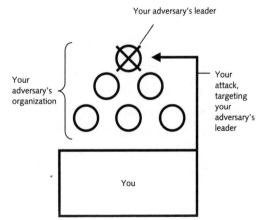

TURNING GUCCI'S HEAD We see this tactic used most often during acquisition battles. When company A wants to acquire Company B, it can either offer the highest bid or it can offer something more closely tailored to the desires of Company B's management. This second approach is usually less costly.

By 1998, Gucci, the fashion house, had staged a dramatic recovery from near bankruptcy and experienced a dramatic run-up in profit growth, making it an enviable acquisition target. Two French companies wanted to purchase Gucci: Moet Hennessy Louis Vuitton SA (LVMH) and Pinault-Printemps-Redoute (PPR).

In January 1999, LVMH began collecting shares in Gucci, and Bernard Arnault, LVMH's chairman, embarked on a series of discussions with Gucci's leadership. LVMH ultimately amassed 34.4 percent of Gucci's shares and was poised for a takeover.

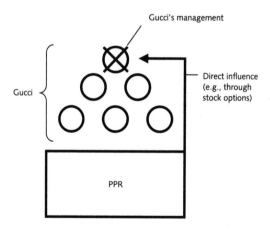

But before LVMH could close in, Gucci announced a deal with PPR. They planned to issue new stock and sell the French retailer forty-two percent of the company. This surprise deal diluted LVMH's holdings to only twenty percent and triggered a two-year struggle for control.

What made the subsequent struggle unique was that management took sides early and passionately instead of waiting for the highest bid. Somehow PPR was able to win Gucci's management over to its side.

Indeed, Gucci's CEO threatened to resign if LVMH took over his company. "No, that's pretty clear . . . I will not stay," he said during an interview.[xiii]

LVMH accused PPR of illegally influencing Gucci's management by issuing stock options to Gucci's CEO and star designer, Tom Ford, that would have vested as soon as a takeover by PPR concluded.

The allegations were never proven. LVMH sued PPR; PPR sued LVMH. In 2001, just before the Dutch court hearing the case was about to give its opinion, PPR, LVMH and Gucci reached a settlement. PPR won the right to buy out Gucci entirely; LVMH received an attractive return on its Gucci investment, and Gucci's CEO kept his job. He and Tom Ford received options; but unlike the previous options, these would not vest until 2004.

Although there was some suspicion that PPR might have acted in an illegal manner, the fact remains that PPR was able to win Gucci's trust thereby winning Gucci's management over. By directing the horse's head, they moved the horse's body, and won the prize.

EXTINGUISHING A SIEGE WITH ONE ARROW In A.D. 756, a city in China's Zhenyuan district was under siege by rebels. The governor of this district was able to hold off the rebels' attacks but unable to turn away their persistent attackers. The governor needed to extinguish the siege permanently, so he decided to implement the stratagem *To catch the bandits, first capture their leader.*

One night, while the rebel army was sleeping, the governor led a surprise attack. His soldiers poured out of the city gates, surprised the rebel soldiers, and killed many of them. In the chaos of battle, however, the governor could not identify the rebel leader. He did not want to claim victory until the leader was found, because if he did, the rebel siege would continue.

To identify the rebel leader, he ordered his archers to use tree branches instead of arrows. The rebels believed by this action that the governor's forces had run out of arrows. Encouraged by this, the rebels reorganized for a counterattack. They assembled around one particular warrior—their leader.

As the rebels prepared for a counterattack, their leader mounted his horse and moved toward the front line. But before the new battle began,

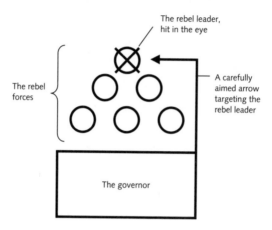

the governor ordered one of his best archers to carefully take aim with a real arrow, not a branch. This arrow hit the rebel leader in his left eye. Immediately losing his will to fight, he ordered a retreat.

SUMMARY Just as PPR apparently guided the entire Gucci organization by influencing Gucci's leadership, the governor of Zhenyuan forced an entire army to retreat by aiming one arrow at his adversary's leader. This arrow achieved what hundreds could not. It ended a persistent siege and saved the city.

The Stratagem of Linking Stratagems

連環計

*When the enemy possesses a superior force, do not
attack recklessly. Instead, weaken him by devising plots to bring him into
a difficult position of his own doing. Good leadership plays a key role in
winning a war. A wise commander gains Heaven's favor.*

—FROM *THE 36 STRATAGEMS*

ACH STRATAGEM, when correctly chosen and executed, can cause
dramatic shifts in power giving its wielder temporary advantage
over her adversaries. But our ambitions—in politics, war, or business—
are longer lasting. Moving from a temporary, one-off advantage to a
continuous or even permanent advantage involves implementing a
stream of linked stratagems. When artfully constructed and incessantly
executed, this stream of stratagems will keep your competition off balance and make you a player few can contend with.

KEY ELEMENTS:

- Rather than execute one strategy,
  you execute multiple ones
  (simultaneously or in succession)

- If one strategy is not effective,
  the next one is. If the next one is
  not effective, the following one is

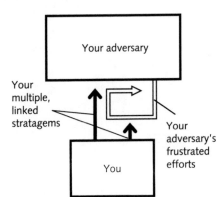

- Your adversary is eventually overwhelmed or caught in an impossible situation, then falls

When able to attack, we must seem unable; when using our forces, we must seem inactive; when we are near, we must make the enemy believe we are far away; when far away, we must make him believe we are near.

Hold out baits to entice the enemy. Feign disorder, and crush him.

If he is secure at all points, be prepared for him. If he is in superior strength, evade him.

If your opponent is of choleric temper, seek to irritate him. Pretend to be weak, that he may grow arrogant.

If he is taking his ease, give him no rest. If his forces are united, separate them.

Attack him where he is unprepared, appear where you are not expected.

—Sun Tzu, *The Art of War*[xiv]

This mode of competition, in which companies attack adversaries with multiple stratagems, each delivering a temporary advantage, is what Richard D'Aveni termed "Hypercompetition." The aim in Hypercompetition is to "hit the competitor from several different directions at once. These approaches leave the competitor harassed or stunned."[xv]

As the cases in this book show, the most competitive companies, such as Coca-Cola, Microsoft, and Sony, maintain their long-term advantage not by executing one superior strategy, not by holding onto a permanent advantage, but rather by unleashing a series of moves (or stratagems) that keep their competition off balance. The sheer number of stratagems they execute and pace at which they do so ensure that while some moves fail, in aggregate these highly competitive companies stay ahead of their peers.

SELLING COLA? Imagine you planned to enter the cola market. Your first step would be to develop a strategy. This strategy would to a large part be predicated on Coca-Cola's strategy. Unfortunately for you, Coca-

Cola does not execute just one strategy. It launches multiple initiatives across the globe and across the beverage value chain (i.e., from sourcing, to bottling, to distribution, to marketing).

- If you achieve some success, Coca-Cola will be close behind you, following each move as it does with Pepsi and Seven-Up (*To catch something, first let it go*). If you happen upon a winning tactic, Coca-Cola will soon be using the same tactic against you.

- If you depend on an ally, Coca-Cola may lure that ally out of your camp, as it did to Pepsi in Venezuela (*The stratagem of sowing discord*)

- If you depend on an input, Coca-Cola may attack the source of that input to hinder your growth, as it attempted to do with high-fructose corn syrup (*Remove the firewood from under the pot*)

- If an opportunity unexpectedly appears, Coca-Cola may move in to take advantage more quickly than you can, as it has done in Latin America and Eastern Europe (*Loot a burning house*)

- Instead of attacking you directly, it may influence a third party to frustrate your efforts, as it did to Monsanto (*Kill with a borrowed knife*)

- If you gain a competitive advantage that Coca-Cola cannot match, it may introduce a new player to the game that can compete with you, just as it created a new "anchor" bottler to compete with Pepsi's bottling operations (*Create something out of nothing*)

Coca-Cola will come at you from many directions and attack multiple parts of your business. Your success will require diligence, persistence, and flexibility.

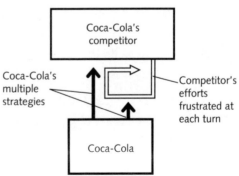

SELLING SOFTWARE? Microsoft is one of the most notoriously strong competitors today. Like Coca-Cola, Microsoft does not limit itself to one strategy. It executes multiple, creative strategies across value chains, markets, and levels (from corporate strategy to operating tactics).

The company's core strategy is *Besiege Wei to rescue Zhao,* which takes the form of one business contributing to the success of another (e.g., Windows contributing to the success of Microsoft's ISP, MSN). But Microsoft executes multiple strategies around this core strategy to confuse, frustrate, and outmaneuver its opponents.

- If you are profitable, Microsoft may sacrifice profits to win consumer loyalty, forcing you to give up your profits as well (*Exchange a brick for a jade*)
- If you command an advantage in your market, it may force you to play a new market, one it knows it can win, as it did to Encyclopedia Britannica (*Lure the enemy onto the roof, then remove the ladder*)
- If you are competing for distribution, Microsoft may use its cash to build influence over distributors as it did to influence retailers to push MSN (*The stratagem of the beautiful woman*)
- Even if you "win" a battle, Microsoft may persist, launching small incursions that build its knowledge of your market and that incrementally erode your lead until it overtakes you (*Beat the grass to startle the snake*)
- If you beat Microsoft to market with an innovation, Microsoft may reveal its intentions to soon make a similar innovation and thus dry up your customers and investors (*The stratagem of the open city gates*)

Competing with Microsoft, like competing with Coca-Cola, demands flexibility. Microsoft is an opponent that will come at you from all directions and that will keep rising from the mat until you are too overwhelmed to continue.

DESIGNER STRATAGEMS Linking stratagems also means combining stratagems to create entirely new ones. This gives us the power to generate nearly endless streams of moves. As Sun Tzu wrote, combining tactics can give rise to "an endless series of maneuvers . . . It is like moving in a circle—you never come to an end. Who can exhaust the possibilities of their combination?" [xvi]

As an example, consider the strategy most promoted by business strategists: pursuing an approach that our competitors will not copy because copying it would expose our competitor to attack from other players in the market. This is the explanation often given for the successes of strategically innovative companies such as Southwest Airlines and Ikea, the furniture store chain.

The 36 Stratagems would explain this strategy as being a combination of two stratagems: (1) *Clamor in the east; attack to the west* and (2) *Kill with a borrowed knife*. First, we attack our competitor in a way

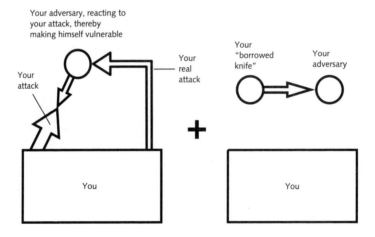

such that in defending himself he exposes himself to another attack (*Clamor in the east; attack to the west*). Then, rather than attack our exposed competitor, we let other players attack him (*Kill with a borrowed knife*). If our competitor defends himself against our attack, he will be attacked by other players in his industry, weakening him and potentially forcing him to call off his defense against us. If our competitor decides that this makes it not worth defending against our incursion, we can move in unhindered. Either way, we win.

THREE GENERALS, THREE STRATEGIES The prince of Chu was being held prisoner by the state of Qi when his father died. He naturally wanted to return home to claim his throne. But the king of Qi demanded a high price for freedom: the prince of Chu, soon to be the king of Chu, would have to give up great stretches of Chu's eastern lands to the kingdom of Qi. The prince reluctantly agreed.

After returning to his home and taking the throne, the new king of Chu faced a dilemma. A regiment of Qi soldiers had approached the Chu border demanding that the king make good on his promise and surrender the eastern lands. The king was unsure how he should deal with his promise—whether he should fulfill it or not. So he summoned three of his generals to ask their advice.

The first general believed the king's only option was to give up the land and later attempt to recapture it. He argued that a king's ability to rule depends on his reputation. If the king proved his word of no value by refusing to give up the eastern lands, his authority would be jeopardized. This general offered to travel to the Qi regiment on the Chu border and surrender the land.

The second general argued that the king should defend the land because it was too large a parcel to give up at any cost. The state's strength depends on its size, so giving up so much would be a disservice to the king's people even if it cost him some face. The general offered to lead troops to defend Chu's eastern borders.

The third general argued that Chu should seek an ally to help defend the land. He agreed with the second general that the land was too large to give up but feared Chu was too weak to prevent Qi from taking it. He offered to lead a diplomatic mission to a large neighboring state, Qin, to request help defending Chu's eastern land.

The king thanked the generals for their advice and dismissed them.

He thought about his three options and decided not to choose between them. Rather, he decided to pursue them all.

The next day, the king ordered the first general to do as he had suggested, and travel to the Qi regiment waiting on the Chu border and announce to them Chu's intention to give up the land promised. The general was pleased and left with a contingent of soldiers.

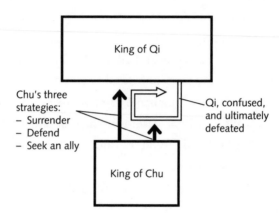

The following day, the king told the second general that he agreed with that general's advice; the land was too high a cost just to keep a king's word. He ordered this general to follow his own suggestion and lead troops toward Chu's eastern border to prepare to defend against an attack from Qi.

On the third day after his initial consultation with the three generals, the king told the third general to do as that general had suggested, and to lead a diplomatic mission to neighboring Qin requesting assistance. This general assembled a small mission and set off for Qin.

The Qi were confused by the mixed messages they were getting from Chu's actions. One Chu general had approached them to surrender the land. But a day later, a second general was preparing to defend it. They decided it was time to bring certainty to their situation, so they sent for reinforcements and planned to take Chu's eastern lands by force.

When Qi's reinforcements arrived, the king of Qi was with them. He had planned to lead his army into battle himself.

As Qi's and Chu's forces lined up opposite each other and prepared to converge, the third general appeared. He was escorting Qin troops, led by a Qin general, who were ready to join forces with Chu.

Outnumbered, the king of Qi called off his attack. The Chu's eastern lands were preserved.[xvii]

SUMMARY Just as Microsoft and Coca-Cola keep their adversaries off-balance and win more consistently by unleashing multiple initiatives, the king of Chu confused his adversary (the king of Qi) and put multiple chances of winning in place by simultaneously executing three strategies. By launching multiple initiatives we become more difficult to handle. By combining different stratagems to create entirely new ones, we become almost impossible to predict.

Permissions

Notes

PART ONE—YIN YANG: POLARITY

i. Sun Tzu, *The Art of War*, chapter 1, paragraph 7; translation from *The Art of War, The Denma Translation* (Boston: Shambhala Classics, 2001), 128–129.

ii. "Can Microsoft Beat Sony and Nintendo at their Own Game?," *Barron's*, May 14, 2001, 25.

iii. Gracian, Baltasar, *The Art of Worldly Wisdom*, translated by Christopher Maurer. (New York: Doubleday, 1992), 47.

iv. Machiavelli, Nicolo, *The Prince*, translated by W. K. Marriott. (www.ilt.columbia.edu/publications/digitext.html)

v. Enrico, Roger, *The Other Guy Blinked and Other Dispatches From the Cola Wars* (New York: Bantam Books, 1988)

vi. Sun Tzu, *The Art of War*, chapter 7, paragraph 36, translated by R. L. Wing as *The Art of Strategy, A New Translation of Sun Tzu's Classic The Art of War* (New York: Doubleday, 1988)

vii. Lao Tzu, *Tao Te Ching*, chapter 78, translated by James Legge (http://classics.mit.edu//Lao/taote.html)

viii. Sun Tzu, *The Art of War*, chapter 11, paragraph 20, translated by Lionel Giles (http://classics.mit.edu//Tzu/artwar.html)

ix. Tichy, Noel M., *Control Your Destiny or Someone Else Will* (New York: Harper Business, 2001), 276

x. "The World on a Disc," *The Guardian*, February 17, 1994

xi. "Toy Soldiers: Can Microsoft Beat Sony and Nintendo at their own Game?," *Barron's*, May 14, 2001

xii. "The Making of the Xbox," *Wired Magazine*, November 2001

xiii. Branson, Richard, *Losing My Virginity* (London: Virgin Publishing 1998), 489

xiv. Sun Tzu, *The Art of War*, chapter 6, paragraph 5, translated by Giles

xv. Sun Tzu, *The Art of War*, translated by Giles

xvi. "The Venezuelan Cola Wars," *Financial Times*, August 20, 1996

Notes

PART TWO — WU WEI: GO WITH THE GRAIN

i. Winston Churchill, speech to the Harrow School on October 29, 1941 (www.winstonchurchill.org/never.htm)

ii. Sun Tzu, *The Art of War*, chapter 4, paragraph 11; translated by Giles

iii. Sun Tzu, *The Art of War*, chapter 9, paragraphs 29 and 30, translated by Giles

iv. Sun Tzu, *The Art of War*, chapter 5, paragraph 4, translated by Giles

v. Ibid., chapter 10, paragraph 18

vi. Musashi, Miyamoto, *The Book of Five Rings*, translated by Thomas Cleary, (Boston: Shambhala, 1993), 41–42

vii. Gracian, Baltasar, *The Art of Worldly Wisdom*, translated by Maurer, 93

viii. Sun Tzu, *The Art of War*, chapter 1, paragraph 19, from The Denma Translation, 132

ix. Sun Tzu, *The Art of War*, chapter 6, paragraph 31, translated by Giles

x. Tichy, Noel M., *Control Your Destiny or Someone Else Will*, (New York: Harper Business, 2001), 98

xi. Sun Tzu, *The Art of War*, chapter 4, paragraphs 1 and 2; translated by Giles

xii. Dearlove, Des, *Business the Bill Gates Way* (New York: AMACOM, 1999), 77

xiii. Branson, Richard, *Losing My Virginity* (London: Virgin Publishing 1998), 211

xiv. "Business: Behind Branson," *Economist*, February 21, 1998, 63

xv. Gracian, Baltasar, *The Art of Worldly Wisdom*, translated by Maurer, 135–136

PART THREE — WU CHANG: CONTINUOUS CHANGE

i. Gracian, Baltasar, *The Art of Worldly Wisdom*, translated by Maurer, 135–136

ii. Popular folktale, originally from *Huai Nan Tzu*; adapted from: Watts, Alan, *Tao, The Watercourse Way* (New York: Pantheon Books, 1975), 31

iii. Lao Tzu, *Tao Te Ching*, chapter 43; translation from R.L. Wing, *The Tao of Power*, (New York: Doubleday, 1986)

iv. Mao Tse-tung, *On Guerilla Warfare*, translated by Samuel B. Griffith II (Urbana and Chicago: University of Illinois Press, 1961), 52

v. Jay Greene, Steve Hamm, Catherine Yang, and Irene M. Kunii, "On to the Living Room! Can Microsoft Control the Digital Home?" *Business Week Magazine,* January 21, 2002.

vi. Marilyn Much "Executive Update Taking on the Goliaths: Virgin Enters Cola Wars," *Investors Business Daily,* September 10, 1996, p. A4.

vii. Adam Brandenburger and Barry Nalebuff, "The Right Game," *Harvard Business Review,* July-August 1995, p. 49.

viii. Gracian, Baltasar, *The Art of Worldly Wisdom*, chapter 99, translation (www.hive.com/books/gracian.html#Paragraphs)

ix. Sun Tzu, *The Art of War,* chapter 6, paragraph 1, from *The Denma Translation*, 158

x. Sam Walton with John Huey, *Made in America* (New York: Bantam Books, 1993), 140.

xi. Gracian, Baltasar, *The Art of Wordly Wisdom*, translated by Maurer, 3

xii. Machiavelli, Nicolo, *The Prince,* chapter 9, translated by Marriott

xiii. "Legend in the Making," *Economist*, September 15, 2001.

xiv. Andrew Tanzer, "A Legend in the Making," *Forbes Magazine*, March 9, 1998.

xv. Machiavelli, Nicolo, *The Prince*, chapter 21, translated by Marriott

xvi. Sun Tzu, *The Art of War*, chapter 21, paragraph 33, from *The Denma Translation*, 205

xvii. Lao Tzu, *Tao Te Ching*, translated by R. L. Wing as *The Tao of Power* (New York: Doubleday, 1986), Chapter 36

PART FOUR—SHANG BING WU BING: INDIRECT ACTION

i. Sun Tzu, *The Art of War,* from *The Denma Translation,* 142

ii. Sun Tzu, *The Art of War,* from *The Denma Translation,* 143.

iii. Sun Tzu, *The Art of War,* translated by Giles

iv. Samuel B. Griffith II, introduction to his translation of *On Guerrilla Warfare*, by Mao Tse-Tung (Urbana: University of Illinois Press, 1961) 26

v. Sun Tzu, *The Art of War*, chapter 1, paragraph 24, translated by Giles

vi. Munenori, Yagyu, *The Book of Family Traditions on the Art of War*, included in Miyamoto Musashi, *The Book of Five Rings*, translated by Cleary, 70

vii. Adapted from Sun Haichen, *The Wiles of War: 36 Military Strategies from Ancient China,* 1–2 and von Senger, *The Book of Stratagems*, 16–17

viii. Sun Tzu, *The Art of War,* chapter 4, paragraph 7, translated by Giles

ix. "The Inside Story," *Rose Hulman Echos,* publication of the Rose-Hulman Institute of Technology, Fall 1997

x. "The Inside Story," *Rose Hulman Echos,* publication of the Rose-Hulman Institute of Technology, Fall 1997

xi. "Hewlett-Packard and MasterCard Join Digital Identity Alliance," *Wireless News*, December 20, 2001

xii. "ID case shows how rivals gain against Microsoft," *The New York Times*, June 4, 2002

xiii. "Gucci's CEO Threatens to Resign if LVMH's Takeover Succeeds," *Asian Wall Street Journal*, March 24, 1999.

xiv. Sun Tzu, *The Art of War*, chapter 1, translated by Giles

xv. D'Aveni, *Hypercompetition*, 280.

xvi. Sun Tzu, *The Art of War*, chapter 5, translated by Giles

xvii. Adapted from: Verstappen, *The Thirty-Six Strategies of Ancient China*, 186–188

Using The 36 Stratagems
as Brainstorming Tools

THIS BOOK IS meant to be used, more than read. It proposes that *The 36 Stratagems* offers thirty-six universal patterns of strategic inter-action, or power moves to create advantage that you can use to sieze advantage.

By first understanding these patterns, then using them as templates with which to structure brainstorming (using visual depictions of the stratagems as aids), we can systematically generate creative, out-of-the-box strategies or solutions to your problems.

STEP 1: DEFINE THE PROBLEM To ensure that our problem-solving process remains focused and efficient, you must clearly articulate the problem we want to solve. This requires defining three elements:

- Situation
- Objective
- Key players (you, your adversary, others)

Defining the *situation* means briefly describing what brought you to the problem at hand. It should be complete but brief (one sentence). Some examples are:

- A new player has entered our market and is eroding our market share
- Growth is slowing in our market

- We want to expand into the XYZ market but this market is dominated by a powerful player

Defining the *objective* means to clearly and briefly articulate either the question you want to answer (e.g., "How can we hinder Acme Company's entrance into our market?") or the goal you want to achieve (e.g., "Acme Company's efforts to enter our market stall, giving us a one-year lead.").

Defining the *players* means simply stating who you are (e.g., "ABC Company"), who your adversary is (e.g., "Acme Company"), and listing any other key player in your game (e.g., "XYZ regulatory agency"). Your adversary does not necessarily need to be your competitor. Your adversary can be any player in your game whose actions you want to influence. It may, for example, be your customer. You may find that you want to specify more than one adversary—your customers and your chief competitor, for example.

STEP 2: GENERATE OPTIONS Here is where you turn to the questions in this appendix. Pick a stratagem at random or in order. For each stratagem you will already know your situation, objective, and players. The questions associated with each stratagem will prompt additional questions that will trigger your creativity and generate new options. Log these options down. Paper, white board, or a flipchart are good tools to use. Capture them quickly and resist the temptation to critique them.

STEP 3: PRIORITIZE YOUR OPTIONS Here you should go through the options you generated in step 2 and highlight the ones you find offer the greatest potential for impact and/or to be easy to implement. You might grade each *A, B,* or *C,* with *A* being high potential and easy to implement, *C* being low potential and difficult to implement, and *B* being everything else.

STEP 4: ANALYZE YOUR OPTIONS Do not act immediately. The process has so far been fact-free. You should now put facts behind your high-priority options (as identified in step 3). The analysis and facts you need depend on the option you are considering and the level of confidence you want to have before you make a decision.

BEGIN The rest of this appendix assumes you have conducted step 1, defining the problem. The stratagems contain the visual description of each, its translation, its key elements, and a few questions to prod your thinking. Let your hair down and open your mind. Now is the time to set aside judgment and have fun!

Note: Visit www.artofadvantage.com for more tools and help with sucessfully applying the 36 stratagems.

Stratagem 1: To catch something, first let it go

> *Press the enemy force too hard and they will strike back fiercely. Let them go and their morale will sink. Follow them closely, but do not push them too hard. Tire them and sap their morale. Then you will be able to capture them without shedding blood. In short, a careful delay in attack will help bring victory.*
>
> —FROM *THE 36 STRATAGEMS*

KEY ELEMENTS:

- You "capture" your enemy
- Though you are able, you do not kill your enemy

IMPLEMENTATION QUESTIONS:

- Who is your adversary?
- What innovations could he introduce (list the 3–5 most likely and significant)?
- Assuming he makes each innovation, what action would you need to have taken to be able to quickly catch up?

Stratagem 2: Exchange a brick for a jade

Use a bait to lure the enemy and take him in.

—FROM *THE 36 STRATAGEMS*

KEY ELEMENTS:

- You give your adversary something on which you place relatively little value
- In exchange, your adversary gives you something you value much more

IMPLEMENTATION QUESTIONS:

- Who is your adversary (e.g., customer, competitor, supplier)?
- What do you have that your adversary values more highly than you do?
- What does your adversary have that he values less than you do?
- What could you exchange each of these "things" for? How could you exchange each?

Stratagem 3: Invite your enemy onto the roof, then remove the ladder

Expose your weak points deliberately to entice the enemy to penetrate into your line, then surround him by cutting off his exit.

—FROM *THE 36 STRATAGEMS*

KEY ELEMENTS:

- You entice your adversary to enter your area of control
- You cut off your adversary's and your soldiers' escape routes
- This motivates your soldiers . . .
- . . . and disadvantages your adversary

IMPLEMENTATION QUESTIONS:

- Who is your opponent?
- What could your "roof" in this stratagem represent (e.g., your product segment, your market)?
- How could you entice your opponent to climb onto your roof?
- What does it mean to "take away the ladder"?
- What would be the impact of executing the resulting strategies?

Stratagem 4: Lure the tiger down from the mountain

> *Use unfavorable natural conditions to trap the enemy in a difficult position. Use deception to lure him out. In an offensive that involves great risk, lure the enemy to come out against you.*
>
> —FROM *THE 36 STRATAGEMS*

KEY ELEMENTS:

- Your adversary is in a stronghold
- You lure your adversary out of this stronghold
- You either (1) attack on open ground or (2) attack the stronghold

IMPLEMENTATION QUESTIONS:

- Who is your adversary?
- What is his stronghold (e.g., market niche, capability)?
- What could your adversary leaving his stronghold look like (e.g., entering XYZ market niche, building ABC capacity)?
- Putting yourself in your adversary's shoes, what would induce your adversary to leave his stronghold?
- In each scenario above, how could you win an advantage from your adversary leaving his stronghold?

Stratagem 5: Befriend the distant enemy to attack one nearby

It is more advantageous to conquer nearby enemies, because of geographical reasons, than those far away. So ally yourself temporarily with your distant enemies in spite of political differences.

—FROM *THE 36 STRATAGEMS*

KEY ELEMENTS:

- You ally with a distant enemy
- You attack a nearby enemy

IMPLEMENTATION QUESTIONS:

- List as many adversaries or types of adversaries as you can
- For each, identify at least one common objective you share
- Classify each adversary or type of adversary according to the degree to which its interests align with yours (i.e., high, medium, or low alignment)
- How might you cooperate or ally yourself with each adversary/type of adversary?
- Who would you jointly attack?
- What would you jointly achieve?

Stratagem 6: Kill with a borrowed knife

Your enemy's situation is clear but your ally's stand is uncertain. At this time, induce your ally to attack your enemy in order to preserve your strength. In dialectic terms, another man's loss is your gain.

—FROM *THE 36 STRATAGEMS*

KEY ELEMENTS:

- You induce a third party to attack your enemy

- You take no direct action
- You influence your adversary with a third party

IMPLEMENTATION QUESTIONS:

- Who are your adversary's adversaries? Have you considered suppliers, distributors, substitutes, competitors?
- What sources of influence do you have over each of these third parties (list as many sources as you can for each)?
- How could you use these sources to influence these third parties to attack your adversary?

Stratagem 7: Besiege Wei to rescue Zhao

It is wiser to launch an attack against the enemy force when they are dispersed than to fight them when they are concentrated. He who strikes first fails and he who strikes late prevails.

—FROM *THE 36 STRATAGEMS*

KEY ELEMENTS:

- You are in direct conflict with an adversary
- Your ally defends you by attacking your adversary
- Your adversary disengages from its conflict with you to defend itself
- Your adversary must now fight on two fronts (this multiplies your chances of success)

IMPLEMENTATION QUESTIONS:

- Other than you, who else is your adversary concerned with? Who else can influence your adversary's success? (List as many as you can.)
- Have you considered competitors or your other divisions/businesses?
- How could these "allies" attack your adversary or complicate his efforts?

- How would your adversary respond?

Stratagem 8: The stratagem of sowing discord

Use the enemy's spies to work for you and you will win without any loss inflicted on your side.

—FROM *THE 36 STRATAGEMS*

KEY ELEMENTS:

- You induce your adversary's agent to work in your favor
- You use this agent to topple a critical relationship on which your adversary depends

IMPLEMENTATION QUESTIONS:

- What critical relationships does your adversary depend on? (List as many as you can.)
- How could you influence or remove each of these relationships?
- What would be the implications of following each course of action?

Stratagem 9: Trouble the water to catch the fish

When the enemy falls into internal chaos, exploit his weakened position and lack of direction and win him over to your side. This is as natural as people going to bed at the end of the day.

—FROM *THE 36 STRATAGEMS*

KEY ELEMENTS:

- You create confusion around your adversary
- This blinds your adversary and so hinders his ability to understand your intentions or see your approach

IMPLEMENTATION QUESTIONS:

- What action would you take if your adversary were too "confused" to react?

- What elements of your adversary's environment—or how he perceives his environment—can you influence?

- How would you influence these elements?

Stratagem 10: Remove the firewood from under the pot

When confronted with a powerful enemy, do not fight them head-on but try to find their weakest spot to initiate their collapse. This is the weak overcoming the strong.

—FROM *THE 36 STRATAGEMS*

KEY ELEMENTS:

- Rather than engage your adversary head-on, you attack his source of power

- This weakens your adversary or hinders his ability to attack

- You defeat your weakened adversary

IMPLEMENTATION QUESTIONS:

- What are your adversary's sources of power? What inputs does your adversary depend on?

- Describe how you could limit your adversary's access to each source or input.

- Which of these methods of influence are most promising?

- What would be their impact?

Stratagem 11: Shut the door to capture the thief

When dealing with a small and weak enemy, surround and destroy him.

If you let him retreat, you will be at a disadvantage in pursuing him.

—FROM *THE 36 STRATAGEMS*

KEY ELEMENTS:

- You encounter a moment when your opponent is weak, divided, or dispersed
- You capitalize on this moment by surrounding your enemy, preventing escape, but avoid direct attack

IMPLEMENTATION QUESTIONS:

- What actions do you want to prevent your adversary from taking? What threat does he pose?
- What sources of influence do you have on your adversary?
- How might you use these sources of influence to contain your adversary (i.e., prevent him from taking action)?
- What would be the outcome of this approach?

Stratagem 12: Replace the beams with rotten timbers

Make the allied forces change their battle formation frequently so that their main strength will be taken away. When they collapse by themselves, go and swallow them up. This is like pulling back the wheels of a chariot to control its direction.

—FROM *THE 36 STRATAGEMS*

KEY ELEMENTS:

- Your adversary's advantage is built on key support structures
- You attack these structures
- By breaking his key support structures, your adversary's integrity falters; then you take him

IMPLEMENTATION QUESTIONS:

- What are your adversary's key support structures? If your adversary is a house, what are his beams?
- How could you attack these support structures or beams?
- What would be the outcome of each attack?
- Which attack seems most promising?

Stratagem 13: The stratagem of the beautiful woman

> *When faced with a formidable enemy, try to subdue their leader. When dealing with an able and resourceful commander, exploit his indulgence of sensual pleasures in order to weaken his fighting spirit. When the commander becomes inept, his soldiers will demoralize, and their combat power will be greatly weakened. This stratagem takes advantage of the enemy's weakness for the sake of self-protection.*
>
> —FROM *THE 36 STRATAGEMS*

KEY ELEMENTS:

- Your adversary has a weakness or need
- You bait your adversary by feeding this weakness or need
- This encourages your adversary to act in a way counter to his benefit
- You take advantage of his misstep

IMPLEMENTATION QUESTIONS:

- What does your adversary want or need? What could the "beautiful woman" represent?
- How could you provide what your adversary needs?
- How could you gain influence over him in providing it?
- What would be the likely outcome of each course of action?

Stratagem 14: Beat the grass to startle the snake

Any suspicion about the enemy's circumstances must be investigated. Before any military action, be sure to ascertain the enemy's situation; repeated reconnaissance is an effective way to discover the hidden enemy.

—FROM *THE 36 STRATAGEMS*

KEY ELEMENTS:

- You are unsure of your enemy's strength or strategy
- You launch a small-scale or indirect attack on your adversary
- Your adversary reveals his strength or strategy by his response to your "false" attack
- You plan your "real" attack with this new knowledge

IMPLEMENTATION QUESTIONS:

- What would a full-scale, committed attack look like?
- What would a small-scale, uncommitted attack look like?
- What new information could you acquire from a small-scale attack? What question might you be able to answer?
- Describe the possible outcomes of a full-scale attack and a small-scale attack.
- Which would you prefer?

Stratagem 15: Loot a burning house

When the enemy falls into severe crisis, exploit his adversity and attack by direct confrontation. This is the strong defeating the weak.

—FROM *THE 36 STRATAGEMS*

KEY ELEMENTS:

- Trouble strikes

- Your adversary freezes or retreats
- You capitalize on your adversary's inaction or retreat to build power

IMPLEMENTATION QUESTIONS:

- What types of trouble create opportunities for you? (List the top five or ten.)
- What opportunities would each of these troubles offer?
- Are you prepared to seize on these opportunities? If not, what would you need to do to be prepared?
- Which troubles are most likely to occur?
- Which might you be able to cause?

Stratagem 16: Sometimes running away is the best strategy

To avoid combat with a powerful enemy, the whole army should retreat and wait for the right time to advance again. This is not inconsistent with normal military principles.

—FROM *THE 36 STRATAGEMS*

KEY ELEMENTS:

- You face a powerful adversary
- You retreat
- You exert your preserved power somewhere else or at some other time

IMPLEMENTATION QUESTIONS:

- Describe what a retreat would mean for you.
- What resources (e.g., money, management time) would a retreat free up?
- What else could you use those resources for?

- What would be the outcome of doing so?

Stratagem 17: Seize the opportunity to lead the sheep away

Exploit any minor lapses on the enemy side, and seize every advantage to your side. Any negligence of the enemy must be turned into a benefit for you.

—FROM *THE 36 STRATAGEMS*

KEY ELEMENTS:

- Your adversary fails to act (e.g., because he is distracted)
- You take advantage of this "deer in the headlights" moment to advance
- By the time your adversary realizes his mistake you have already taken the advantage

IMPLEMENTATION QUESTIONS:

- If you were your adversary, what opportunities or initiatives would you be pursuing right now? What would be on your agenda?
- Is your adversary acting on all of these?
- For those he is not acting on, why do you think he is not acting?
- What opportunity might his inaction offer you?

Stratagem 18: Feign madness but keep your balance

At times, it is better to pretend to be foolish and do nothing than to brag about yourself and act recklessly. Be composed and plot secretly, like thunder clouds hiding themselves during winter only to bolt out when the time is right.

—FROM *THE 36 STRATAGEMS*

KEY ELEMENTS:

- Your adversary is powerful and/or you are weak

- You appear mad or incapable in order to avoid being perceived as a threat

- When your adversary puts down his guard, you take him

IMPLEMENTATION QUESTIONS:

- What reaction (i.e., to your plans) do you want to prevent?

- What would your adversary need to believe about you to choose not to react? What does appearing to be "mad" mean in your context?

- How might you get your adversary to believe you are mad? (e.g., could you change something about your plan to appear "mad")?

- What would be the likely outcome of each approach identified?

Stratagem 19: Watch the fire on the other shore

> *When a serious conflict breaks out within the enemy alliance, wait quietly for the chaos to build. Because once its internal conflict intensifies, the alliance will bring destruction upon itself. As for you, observe closely and make preparations for any advantage that may come from it.*
>
> —FROM *THE 36 STRATAGEMS*

KEY ELEMENTS:

- Your adversary is engaged in internal conflict or in conflict with his allies

- Your attack might unify your adversary (and his allies)

- You refrain from acting

- Allowed to continue, the conflict damages your adversary

IMPLEMENTATION QUESTIONS:

- What is your current battle?

- What might your next battle be?

- What would happen if you engaged in this battle? Would your adversary become stronger or weaker; would you be more or less prepared for the next battle?

- What would happen if you refrained from acting in this battle? Would your adversary become stronger or weaker; would you be more or less prepared for the next battle?

- How can you be better prepared for the next battle?

Stratagem 20: Let the plum tree wither in place of the peach

When loss is inevitable, sacrifice the part for the benefit of the whole.

—FROM *THE 36 STRATAGEMS*

KEY ELEMENTS:

- You cannot win on all fronts

- You allow your adversary a victory on one front

- You preserve, even strengthen, another front

- With this preserved front, you defeat your adversary

IMPLEMENTATION QUESTIONS:

- What are the "fronts" of your battle?

- For one of these fronts, what would your sacrifice be?

- What would be the positive and negative implications of such a sacrifice?

- Describe the net outcome of pursuing a sacrifice on each of your fronts. Write a one paragraph description of the situation each sacrifice would lead to.

- Does a sacrifice on one of these fronts put you in a better position than battling on all fronts?

Stratagem 21: the Stratagem of the open city gates

In spite of the inferiority of your force, deliberately make your defensive line defenseless in order to confuse the enemy. In situations when the enemies are many and you are few, this tactic seems all the more intriguing.

—FROM *THE 36 STRATAGEMS*

KEY ELEMENTS:

- Your adversary is attacking or preparing to do so
- You reveal your strength or weakness
- Your adversary calls off his attack because he fears your strength or no longer considers you a threat (he views you as weak)

IMPLEMENTATION QUESTIONS:

- List as many adversaries as you can (e.g., direct competitors, suppliers, distributors.)
- If you revealed your true strategy to your adversary, would he view you as a strong or weak threat? (Answer for each adversary identified.)
- How would he react to this knowledge? (Answer for each adversary identified.)
- Given the answers above, should you reveal your strategy or plans?
- How would you want him to act?
- What information would induce him to act that way?

Stratagem 22: Await the exhausted enemy at your ease

To weaken the enemy, it is not necessary to attack him directly. Tire him by carrying out an active defense and in so doing his strength will be reduced and your side will gain the upper hand.

—FROM *THE 36 STRATAGEMS*

KEY ELEMENTS:

- You predict the battleground will shift
- You set up a defendable position on the new battleground
- You wait for your adversary
- When your adversary arrives you use your superior position to defeat him

IMPLEMENTATION QUESTIONS:

- Who is your adversary?
- How does he define the battlefield?
- To where might the battlefield shift? (List as many possibilities as you can.)
- Why might the battlefield shift (for each possibility given above)?
- Which shift is most likely to happen?
- What actions could you take to prepare for this shift or to be there already when it does shift?
- What actions could you take to accelerate this shift?

Stratagem 23: Exchange the role of guest for that of host

> *Whenever there is a chance, enter into the decision-making body of your ally and extend your influence skillfully step by step. Eventually, put it under your control.*

—FROM *THE 36 STRATAGEMS*

KEY ELEMENTS:

- Your adversary accepts you as unthreatening
- You incrementally build power over your adversary
- You take control

IMPLEMENTATION QUESTIONS:

- Who is your adversary?
- What levers exert control over him (e.g., his capacity, access to funding, customer relationships)? List at least five.
- What might trigger a defensive action from him?
- What weak position could you take now to prevent such a defensive action?
- How could you build on this position to begin controlling the levers you identified above? List at least five.
- Of the strategies identified (levers, new positioning, plan to control levers), which is most attractive?

Stratagem 24: Borrow the road to conquer Gao

> When a small state, located between two big states, is being threatened by the enemy state, you should immediately send troops to rescue it, thereby expanding your sphere of influence. Mere talk cannot win the trust of a state in a difficult position.
>
> —FROM *THE 36 STRATAGEMS*

KEY ELEMENTS:

- You share a common objective or enemy with another
- You form an alliance to achieve this objective
- You then take your ally

IMPLEMENTATION QUESTIONS:

- What is your objective?
- What skill or capability are you missing to achieve this objective?
- What partners could get you what you are missing and what shared objective would bring you together? List at least five.

- For each partner listed above, what actions could you take to ensure you will not need your partner in the future?
- Which option (combination of partner and actions) yields the most attractive outcome?

Stratagem 25: Shed your skin like the golden secada

Make your front array appear as if you are still holding your position so that the allied force will not suspect your intention and the enemy troops will not dare to attack rashly. Then withdraw your main forces secretly.

—FROM *THE 36 STRATAGEMS*

KEY ELEMENTS:

- You establish a façade
- Your adversary focuses on your façade confusing it for the real action
- You move the real action somewhere else

IMPLEMENTATION QUESTIONS:

- Who are your adversaries, or what threats must you contend with? (List as many as possible.)
- What attracts these adversaries or threats?
- What façade could you create to hide from your adversaries?
- Where could you "move the action" so as to prevent your adversaries from noticing?

Stratagem 26: The stratagem of injuring yourself

People rarely inflict injuries on themselves, so when they get injured, it is usually genuine. Exploit this naivety to make the enemy believe your words; then sowing discord within enemy will work. In this case, one takes advantage of the enemy's weakness, and makes the enemy look as if he were a naive child easily taken.

—FROM *THE 36 STRATAGEMS*

KEY ELEMENTS:

- Your adversary's suspicion hinders your success
- You injure yourself either (1) to win your adversary's trust or (2) to avoid appearing to be a threat
- Your adversary accepts you or lets down his guard
- You take advantage of this opening by attacking your adversary

IMPLEMENTATION QUESTIONS:

- Who is your adversary? (List as many as possible.)
- What is your objective?
- How and why is your adversary hindering you (for each adversary identified)?
- If you appeared less threatening would he stop hindering you?
- How could you "injure" yourself to appear less threatening?
- What would be the outcome of such an action (for both this game and the next)?

Stratagem 27: Borrow a corpse for the soul's return

The powerful is beyond exploitation, but the weak needs help. Exploit and manipulate the weak for they need you more than you need them.

—FROM *THE 36 STRATAGEMS*

The practiced definition of this stratagem means to pick up the dead or forgotten.

KEY ELEMENTS:

- You adopt something forgotten/abandoned (a model, idea, or technology)
- Because your adversaries have abandoned it, only you use this thing
- You convert this uniqueness into power

IMPLEMENTATION QUESTIONS:

- What models, ideas, or technologies have your competitors abandoned?
- For each of the above, describe what would happen if you readopted it.
- Would you differentiate yourself?
- How would competitors respond?
- Should you readopt any of these models, ideas, or technologies?

Stratagem 28: Point at the mulberry but curse the locust

> *When the powerful wants to rule over the weak, he will sound a warning. One's uncompromising stand will often win loyalty, and one's resolute action, respect.*

> —FROM *THE 36 STRATAGEMS*

KEY ELEMENTS:

- You want to influence your adversary's behavior
- Rather than attack your adversary directly, you focus your attention on a different target
- This action sends a covert message to your adversary that displays your power and communicates your intention
- Your adversary, appreciating your power and intention, alters his behavior

IMPLEMENTATION QUESTIONS:

- What do you want your adversary to do?

- What messages would induce him to do this? (List as many as possible.)

- What "false attack" might send him this message?

- Who might your "apparent adversary" be for this "false attack"?

Stratagem 29: Clamor in the east; attack to the west

> *When the enemy command is in confusion, it will be unprepared for contingencies. The situation is like flood waters rising higher and higher; likely to burst the dam at any moment. When the enemy loses internal control, take the chance and destroy him.*
>
> —FROM *THE 36 STRATAGEMS*

KEY ELEMENTS:

- You feign an attack

- Your adversary responds to this false attack

- In responding to this attack, your enemy is exposed to your true attack

- You launch your true attack and defeat your adversary

IMPLEMENTATION QUESTIONS:

- What attack does your adversary expect?

- What actions would your adversary take to defend against such an attack?

- In taking these actions, what "real" attack would your adversary expose himself to? (List as many as possible.)

- What would be the outcome of feigning the "false" attack and launching each "real" attack identified?

- How could you reinforce your adversary's expectation of the "false" attack?

Stratagem 30: Openly repair the walkway, secretly march to Chen Cang

> *To pin down the enemy, expose part of your action deliberately, so that you can make a surprise attack somewhere else.*
>
> —FROM *THE 36 STRATAGEMS*

KEY ELEMENTS:

- You focus your adversary, or let your adversary focus, on a direct, orthodox attack
- You launch an indirect, unorthodox attack
- This indirect, unorthodox action surprises your adversary
- You take the advantage

IMPLEMENTATION QUESTIONS:

- What attack (i.e., orthodox attack) does your adversary expect?
- What actions will your adversary likely take to defend against this attack?
- In taking these actions, what "unorthodox" attack would your adversary expose himself to? (List as many as possible.)
- What would be the outcome of feigning the "obvious" attack and launching each "unorthodox" attack?
- How could you reinforce your adversary's expectation of the "obvious" attack?

Stratagem 31: Fool the emperor and cross the sea

> *The perception of perfect preparation leads to relaxed vigilance. Familiar sights lead to slackened suspicion. Therefore, secret machinations are*

better concealed in the open than in the dark, and extreme public exposure often contains extreme secrecy.

—FROM THE 36 STRATAGEMS

KEY ELEMENTS:

- Your adversary is vigilant
- You take actions that appear normal (i.e., that appear to be everyday actions)
- Your adversary fixes his attention on this façade of normalcy. He does not see your true attack or intention
- You take your adversary

IMPLEMENTATION QUESTIONS:

- What attack would you like to launch?
- What normal, everyday occurrences exist in your environment (e.g., stock purchases, real estate purchases)? List as many as you can
- How could you hide your desired attack within these everyday occurrences?

Stratagem 32: Create something out of nothing

Design a counterfeit front to put the enemy off guard. When the trick works, the front is changed into something real so that the enemy will be thrown into a state of double confusion. In short, deceptive appearances often conceal forthcoming danger.

—FROM THE 36 STRATAGEMS

KEY ELEMENTS:

- Your direct attack (i.e., one using existing players) is ineffective

- You create a new player/entity
- This player/entity catches your adversary off guard
- You or the new player/entity take your adversary

IMPLEMENTATION QUESTIONS:

- What would a direct attack (i.e., one using the existing players) look like?
- What new player would improve your chances of success if introduced? (List as many as possible.)
- What would be the impact of each new player being introduced?
- What would it take to introduce each new player?

Stratagem 33: Hide a dagger behind a smile

> *One way or another, make the enemies trust you and thereby slacken their vigilance. Meanwhile, plot secretly, making preparations for your future action to ensure its success.*
>
> —FROM *THE 36 STRATAGEMS*

KEY ELEMENTS:

- A direct attack would generate resistance in your adversary
- You choose an approach that is, or appears to be, friendly
- Your adversary lets down his defenses and welcomes this approach
- You take your adversary with a secondary or hidden attack

IMPLEMENTATION QUESTIONS:

- How would your adversary likely respond to a direct attack?
- What would an apparently "friendly" approach look like?
- What could you do that your adversary would appreciate? What actions would your adversary welcome?

- How might you achieve your objective (i.e., of the direct attack) by taking the actions your adversary would welcome?

- What would be the outcome of this approach?

Stratagem 34: Deck the tree with bogus blossoms

Use deceptive appearances to make your troop formation look more powerful than it is. When wild geese soar high above, the grandness of their formation is greatly enhanced by the display of their outstretched wings.

—FROM *THE 36 STRATAGEMS*

KEY ELEMENTS:

- You are too weak to attack your adversary alone

- You coordinate individual elements within your environment

- Coordinated, these parts become a much stronger whole

- You are now strong enough to defeat your adversary

IMPLEMENTATION QUESTIONS:

- What components are available for you to coordinate? (List as many as possible.)

- What potential allies exist?

- What internal elements compose your organization (e.g., Tian Dan had bulls, woman, children, and warriors)?

- What are the strengths and interests/objectives of each component listed?

- What combination of strengths, if coordinated, would compose a viable opponent for your adversary?

- How could you use each component's interest to induce it to cooperate?

Stratagem 35: To catch the bandits, capture their leader

Capture their chief, and the enemy will collapse. His situation will be as desperate as a sea dragon fighting on land.

—FROM *THE 36 STRATAGEMS*

KEY ELEMENTS:

- You face a persistent adversary
- You identify your adversary's leader or leaders
- You aim your attack on this leader or these leaders
- Your adversary's leadership falls and brings down your adversary's organization with it

IMPLEMENTATION QUESTIONS:

- What do you want your adversary to do?
- Who in your adversary's organization can force your adversary to do this?
- How can you influence this person or these people?

Stratagem 36: The stratagem of linking stratagems

When the enemy possesses a superior force, do not attack recklessly. Instead, weaken him by devising plots to bring him into a difficult position of his own doing. Good leadership plays a key role in winning a war. A wise commander gains Heaven's favor.

—FROM *THE 36 STRATAGEMS*

KEY ELEMENTS:

- Rather than execute one strategy, you execute multiple ones (simultaneously or in succession)

- If one strategy is not effective, the next one is. If the next one is not effective, the following one is

- Your adversary is eventually overwhelmed or caught in an impossible situation and falls

IMPLEMENTATION QUESTIONS:

- Which of the strategies you identified above are your favorites (e.g., which provide the greatest impact with the least effort)?

- Which might you combine? Which could you easily launch simultaneously?

- Which are completely unrelated but could nevertheless be launched simultaneously?

- What stratagems could you combine to create new stratagems?

- What new options do these offer for you?

List of Cases

Master list of cases categorized by stratagem, listing company name and brief text describing either the company's adversary or a description of the case. Not all the cases listed here are included in this book. Those included are listed in the Introduction to the book.

STRAT.	COMPANY	ADVERSARY/DESCRIPTION
1	Barnes & Noble	Borders
1	Barnes & Noble	Amazon.com
1	Bertelsmann	CD-Now acquisition
1	Coca-Cola	Pepsi
1	Dell	Clones IBM computers
1	Estée Lauder	Gloss.com acquisition
1	FedEx	Offers overnight service
1	Gallo	California Wine Cooler
1	IBM	Closely follows competitors
1	Kodak	Sony
1	Matsushita	VHS introduction
1	Microsoft	Converts customers from Word Perfect
1	Proctor Silex	Private label products

STRAT.	COMPANY	ADVERSARY/DESCRIPTION
1	Rohm and Haas	Acetylene industry
1	Seiko	Closely follows watch competitors
1	Seven-Up	Coca-Cola and Pepsi
2	Amazon.com	Customer review program
2	American Airlines	Frequent flier program
2	AOL	Customer acquisition strategy
2	Camera manufacturers	Strategy to create standard
2	Club Med	Ability to pay below-average wages
2	Coca-Cola	Grocery channel as loss leader
2	Coca-Cola	Fountain accounts as loss leader
2	Consumer electronics firms	Profiting from financing business
2	Elevator industry	Profiting from servicing business
2	Gas stations	Leaded gasoline as loss leader
2	GE	Profiting from financing business
2	Gillette	Pricing strategy
2	GM	Introduces credit card
2	Microsoft	Strategy to create standard
2	Pepsi	Fountain accounts as loss leader
2	Virgin	Trades brand value for equity
2	Wireless service providers	Pricing strategy
3	ABB	Corporate structure
3	Mario Gabelli	Management compensation
3	Mercedes-Benz	Listing on U.S. stock exchange

STRAT.	COMPANY	ADVERSARY/DESCRIPTION
3	Microsoft	Encyclopedia Britannica
3	Pepsi	Coca-Cola
3	Procter & Gamble	Management incentives
3	Thermo Electron	Corporate culture
4	Ben & Jerry's	Häagen-Dazs
4	Iowa Beef Packers	Supply chain strategy
5	3DO	Alignment of incentives with partners
5	Anheuser-Busch	Overestimation of synergies value
5	Arctic Cat	Alliance with Suzuki
5	Century 21	Realtor coalitions
5	Corning	Joint venturing policy
5	Intel	Alignment of interests with Dell and Compaq
5	Kellogg	Product mix strategy
5	Lincoln Highway Assoc.	Formed by GM, Goodyear, and Prest-O-Lite
5	Lumberyards	Buying groups
5	Quaker Oats	Snapple acquisition
5	Sears	Overestimation of synergies value
5	Toyota	Supplier alliances
6	Carl Icahn	White Knight
6	Coca-Cola	Home Sweetener Company
6	Cocoa industry	US and EU build African supply
6	European telecom companies	Governmental protection

STRAT.	COMPANY	ADVERSARY/DESCRIPTION
6	Ford	Marketing strategy for Ford Focus
6	Pharmaceutical industry	FDA process
7	Barbie	Low-end protect high-end products
7	Canon	Leveraging optoelectronics capabilities
7	Coca-Cola	Presence building strategy
7	Fox	Uses multiplatform strategy
7	Gillette	Bic
7	Honda	Leveraging motor capabilities
7	Microsoft	Explorer introduction
7	Monsanto	Pricing strategy
7	Seiko	Pulsar acquisition
7	Sharp	Leveraging optoelectronics capabilities
7	Starbucks	Expansion strategy
7	Swatch	Low-end protect high-end products
7	U.S. auto manufacturers	Failed to protect low-end segments in 1960s
8	Amway	Japanese distribution model
8	Avon	Chinese distribution model
8	Coca-Cola	Pepsi's Venezuelan bottler
8	Coca-Cola	Latin American shop owners
8	Enron	Lobbying activities
8	KFC	McDonald's in China
9	Airlines	Pricing strategies
9	Blockbuster	Merchandising strategy

Appendix B

STRAT.	COMPANY	ADVERSARY/DESCRIPTION
9	Coca-Cola	Product bundling
9	Financial trading firms	Product development strategy
9	Hotels	Room bundling
9	Microsoft	Product bundling
9	Starbucks	Value proposition
9	Telephone companies	Pricing strategies
10	Alcoa	Power supply monopolization
10	Coca-Cola	High-fructose corn syrup supply
10	Kirch	Content supply strategy
10	McDonald's	Real estate supply
10	MCI	AT&T
10	Minnetonka	Softsoap pump supply
10	Procter & Gamble	Supermarket display
10	Sony	Columbia Pictures and CBS acquisitions
10	Xerox	Patent strategy
11	Borders	Upsell tactics
11	Gallo	Control over growers and distributors
11	IBM	Distribution strategy
11	Matsushita	Sony/licensing strategy
11	Microsoft	Sun Microsystems
11	Movie studios	Video business
11	Movie theaters	Concession business
11	Nintendo	Software developers

STRAT.	COMPANY	ADVERSARY/DESCRIPTION
11	Peter Pan	Travel business
11	U-Haul	Moving supplies business
12	Bloomberg	Marketing strategy
12	Disney	Use of animated characters
12	Kodak	Polaroid/1 hour processing
12	Sony	Nintendo's game developers
13	McCaw	BellSouth
13	Microsoft	Invests in Best Buy and Radio Shack
14	7–11	Customer information tactics
14	Bristol-Myers	Tylenol
14	Microsoft	Server software entry
14	Yamaha	Listening lab in London
15	Bangladeshi textile industry	Malaysian textile industry
15	Caterpillar	Komatsu
15	Coca-Cola	Pepsi
15	Compac	Alta Vista
15	Deloitte and Touche	PricewaterhouseCoopers
15	Michelin	Internal Rubber
15	Virgin	Japanese entry timing
16	Gallo	Exits low-end jug wine
16	GE	#1, #2, or exit strategy
16	General Dynamics	Gives up F-16 program
16	Intel	Exits memory chips

STRAT.	COMPANY	ADVERSARY/DESCRIPTION
16	Sony	Exits Betamax
16	Virgin	Sells shares to expand
17	AT&T	Enters credit card business
17	Coca-Cola	Attacks water
17	Home Depot	Attacks contractors
17	Intuit	Attacks pencil and paper
17	Microsoft	Overall strategy
17	Sony	Transistor radio development
17	Sony	Attacks Kodak with digital photos
18	Telecom Italia	Olivetti hostile bid
18	Virgin	Enters airline business
19	Burger King	McDonald's
19	Chrysler	Ford and GM
19	Daiwoo	U.K. market
19	Dr. Pepper	Entry into cola market
19	Epson	Entry into laser printer business
19	Gallo	Distribution strategy
19	Ikea	Overall strategy
19	Intel	Non-compete policy
19	Mainstream airlines	Budget airlines
19	Rolls Royce	U.S. entry
19	Virgin	Asia strategy
20	British Airways	Focus on long-haul travel

STRAT.	COMPANY	ADVERSARY/DESCRIPTION
20	De Beers	Overall strategy
20	IBM	RISC chip introduction
20	Intel	Multiple product introduction
20	Morgan Stanley	Focus on large deals
20	Nintendo	16-bit game business
20	Sony	Cannibalization strategy
20	TWA	Removes seats
20	UK grocers	Internet strategy
21	Goodyear	Reveals capacity and strategy
21	Kiwi	Reveals limited aspirations
21	Legend	Transparent corporate reporting
21	Microsoft	Reveals digital home strategy
22	Asahi	Kirin
22	Disney	Maintains non-core businesses
22	H. Wayne Huizenga	Miami Dolphins
22	Microsoft	Software positioning
22	Wal-Mart	Sears
23	7–11 Japan	Acquires U.S. parent
23	Air Products and Chemicals	Industrial gas storage services
23	Ames	Zayre Corporation acquisition
23	Colombian coffee industry	Branding strategy
23	Facset	Transformation to database service
23	Intel	IBM

STRAT.	COMPANY	ADVERSARY/DESCRIPTION
23	Lumberyards	Contractors
23	Microsoft	IBM
23	Nintendo	Strategy of limiting supply
23	Oral B	Replacement indicator
23	Wal-Mart	Foreign manufacturers
23	WorldCom	MCI acquisition
24	Coca-Cola	Follow US troops in WWII
24	DHL	Sinotrans alliance
24	Hershey	Expansion strategy
24	Hindustan-Lever	Unilever alliance
24	InterTrust	AOL
24	Japanese government	Promotes foreign alliances
24	Komatsu	Allies with U.S. firms
24	Legend	HP alliance
24	Michelin	Upward integration
24	Microsoft	Comcast alliance
24	Virgin	Alliances with Asian firms
24	Wal-Mart	Expansion strategy
25	Disney	Book publishing business
25	Kimberly-Clark	Expansion into consumer products
25	Thomson Travel Group	Linked businesses
25	Virgin	Corporate structure
26	American Airlines	On defensive for being too strong

STRAT.	COMPANY	ADVERSARY/DESCRIPTION
26	Apple	IBM
26	Intel	Securing supply contract with IBM
26	Matsushita	Attracts VHS partners
26	Microsoft	On defensive for being too strong
26	Pilkington	Expands glass market
26	Sony	Enters low-end radios
26	Virgin	Entry into U.S. cola market
26	Wal-Mart	On defensive for being too strong
27	Arm and Hammer	Marketing strategy
27	Disney	Re-release of *Snow White*
27	Goodyear	New product development strategy
27	Nucor	Minimill development
27	Perrier	Marketing strategy
27	Southwest Airlines	Point-to-point model
27	U.S. consumer goods manufacturers	Made-to-order production
28	Crazy Eddie	Price guarantee
28	DreamWorks SKG	Marketing strategy for *American Beauty*
28	Kmart	Blue light brand
28	Microsoft	"Vaporware" announcements
28	New York Post	Daily News
28	Polaroid	Strategy of vigorous defense
28	Software developers	New product announcements

Appendix B

STRAT.	COMPANY	ADVERSARY/DESCRIPTION
28	Sony	Columbia Records acquisition
28	Virgin	U.S. Congress lobbying efforts
29	Flick brothers	Feldmühle Nobel
29	Hindustan-Lever	Branding and distribution strategies
29	Microsoft	OS/2 and Windows introductions
29	Pepsi	12 oz. bottle introduction
30	Avon	Limitations of distribution model
30	Body Shop	Franchising strategy
30	Canon	SME distribution strategy
30	First Direct	Overall strategy
30	Hanes	Distribution strategy
30	Hindustan-Lever	Marketing and distribution tactics
30	Japanese car manufacturers	Lift-truck segment entry
30	Polaroid	Kodak
30	U.S. Airlines	Non-price competition
31	Alcoa	Capacity expansion policy
31	Krupp AG	Hoesch acquisition
32	Boeing	Creation of United Airlines
32	Coca-Cola	Creation of independent bottling subsidiary
32	De Beers	Creation of engagement ring tradition
32	Ford	Ownership of Hertz
32	Miller	Lite beer segment creation
32	Pepsi	Food chain business

STRAT.	COMPANY	ADVERSARY/DESCRIPTION
32	Virgin	Branded venture capital strategy
33	Chrysler	Price guarantee
33	GE	Attractiveness as partner
33	IBM	Leasing policy
33	Intel	Branding strategy
33	Japanese car manufacturers	Response to "Buy American" campaign
33	Retailers	Price protection
34	ABB	Corporate structure
34	ACER	Network of alliances
34	Bennetton	Supplier and distributor network
34	Coca-Cola	Bottling network
34	Ford and Chrysler	Supplier networks
34	Liberty Alliance	Microsoft
34	Symbian	Microsoft
34	Virgin	Corporate structure
35	Disney	Touchstone
35	Gucci	Moet Hennessy Louis Vuitton SA (LVMH) and Pinault-Printemps-Redoute (PPR)
35	Philips Electronics	B2B marketing strategy
35	U.S. aluminum industry	Converts steel cans into aluminum
36	Coca-Cola	Multiple
36	Microsoft	Multiple

Bibliography

HISTORICAL SOURCES

Ames, Roger T. (compiler), *The Art of Rulership* (Albany, NY: State University of New York Press, 1994)

Bin, Sun, *Sun Bin Bing Fa,* translated by: Jinjun Xia (Boulder and Oxford: Westview Press, 1995)

Bin, Sun, *The Lost Art of War: Sun Bin's Art of War,* translated by Thomas Cleary (New York: HarperCollins, 1996)

Bozan, Jian, Shao Xunzheng, and Hu Hua, *A Concise History of China* (Beijing: Foreign Language Press, 1981)

Brahm, Laurence J., *Negotiating in China—36 Strategies* (Hong Kong: Haga Group Limited, 1996)

Champion de Crespigny, Richard Rafe, *The Last of the Han* (Canberra, Australia: The Australian National University, 1969)

Chan-Kuo Ts'e (Zhan Guo Ce), translated by: J.R. Crump, Jr. (Oxford: Clarendon Press, 1970)

Chu, Chin-Jing, *The Asian Mind Game* (New York: Scribner, 1991)

Cleary, Thomas, *The Japanese Art of War* (Boston and London: Shambhala, 1992)

Hookham, Hilda, *A Short History of China* (New York and Scarborough, Ontario: The New American Library of Canada Limited, 1972)

Lao Tzu, *The Tao of Power; Lao Tzu's Classic Guide to Leadership, Influence, and Excellence* (New York: Doubleday, 1986)

Legge, James, *The Chinese Classics; Volume V; The Ch'un Ts'ew with The Tso Chuen* (Hong Kong: Hong Kong University Press, 1970)

Machiavelli, Niccolo, *The Prince and Other Political Writings,* (London: Orion Publishing Group, 1995)

Mote, F.W., *Imperial China 900–1800* (Cambridge, MA: Harvard University Press, 1999)

Musashi, Miyamoto, *The Book of Five Rings,* translated by Victor Harris (New York: Woodstock, 1982)

Musashi, Miyamoto; *The Book of Five Rings*, translated by Bradford J. Brown, Yuko Kashiwagi, William H. Barrett, and Eisuke Sasagawa (New York: Bantam Books, 1992)

Pan Ku, *History of the Former Han Dynasty*, translated by: Homer H. Dubs (Baltimore: Waverly Press, 1938)

Pin, Sun, *Sun Pin Military Methods*, translated by Ralph D. Sawyer (Boulder, CO and Oxford, U.K.: Westview Press, 1995)

Sawyer, Ralph D. (translator and compiler), *The Art of the Warrior—Leadership and Strategy from the Chinese Military Classics* (Boston and London: Shambhala, 1996)

Sawyer, Ralph D. with Mei-Chun Lee, *The Six Secret Teachings on the Way of Strategy* (Boston and London: Shambhala, 1997)

Ssu-Ma Ch'ien, *Records of the Grand Historian of China*, compiled by W.M. Theodore de Bary (New York: Columbia University Press, 1968)

Ssu-Ma Ch'ien, *Records of the Grand Historian*, translated by Burton Watson (New York: Columbia University Press, 1995)

Ssu-Mae Ch'ien, *The Grand Scribe's Records; The Basic Annals of Pre-Han China*, translated by Tsai-fa Cheng, Zongli Lu, William H. Nienhauser, Jr., and Robert Reynolds (Bloomington and Indianapolis: Indiana University Press, 1994)

The Han Civilization, translated by K.D. Chang and Zhongshu Wang (New Haven, CT: Yale University Press, 1982)

The Tso Chuan—Selections of China's Oldest Narrative History (*Zuo Zhuan*), translated by Burton Watson (New York: Columbia University Press, 1989)

Three Kingdoms: Chinese Classics, translated by: Luo Guanzhong, Moss Roberts, and Lo Kuan-Chung (Beijing: Foreign Language Press, 2001)

Twitchett, Denis (editor), *The Cambridge History of China* (Cambridge, U.K., New York, and Oakleigh, Melbourne: Cambridge University Press, 1979)

Unorthodox Strategies, translated by Ralph D. Sawyer (New York: Barnes & Noble Books, 1996)

Verstappen, Stefan H., *The Thirty-Six Strategies of Ancient China* (San Francisco: China Books & Periodicals, 1999)

von Senger, Harro, *Stratageme* (Bern, Munich, and Vienna: Scherz Verlag, 2000)

Wee Chow Hou and Lan Luh Luh, *The 36 Strategies of the Chinese* (Singapore: Addison-Wesley, 1998)

Wong, Eva, *The Shambhala Guide to Taoism* (Boston and London: Shambhala, 1997)

Wright, Arthur F., *The Sui Dynasty* (New York: Alfred A. Knopf, 1978)

Wright, David C., *The History of China* (Westport, CT: Greenwood Press, 2001)

Xuanming, Wang, *Thirty-Six Stratagems* (Singapore: Asiapac, 1992)

Bibliography

Zen Flesh, Zen Bones, compiled by Paul Reps and Nyogen Senzaki (Boston and Rutland, VT: Tuttle Publishing, 1998)

HISTORICAL ONLINE SOURCES

www.geocities.com/Area51/Shire/5882/36s.html

http://vikingphoenix.com/public/SunTzu/36biblio.htm

www.chinapage.com/36tact1.html

www.warrior-scholar.com/Warrior-Scholar/Warrior-scholar/Fun/library/36%20strata-gems.html

http://senseis.xmp.net/?SecretArtOfWar

www.geocities.com/auchengyu/strategies

www.thejobfairy.com/sun_tzu/

www.chinastrategies.com

CONTEMPORARY SOURCES

INTRODUCTION

Gleick, James, *Chaos: Making a New Science,* (New York: Penguin Books, 1988)

"Simple Science," *Business Week,* May 27, 2002, and Wolfram, Stephen, *A New Kind of Science* (Champaign, Ill: Wolfram Media 2002)

I. YIN YANG/ POLARITY

Watts, Alan, *Tao, The Watercourse Way* (New York: Pantheon Books, 1975)

Stratagem 1: To catch something, first let it go

Moriguchi, Chiaki, and Lane, David, "A Hundred-Year War: Coke vs. Pepsi, 1890s—1990s," Harvard Business School Case No. 9–799–117, January 14, 2000, p. 6

D'Aveni, Richard, *Hypercompetition* (New York: Free Press, 1994)

Stratagem 2: Exchange a brick for a jade

Norton, Leslie, P. "Toy Soldiers: Can Microsoft Beat Sony and Nintendo at their Own Game?," *Barron's,* May 14, 2001

Takahashi, Dean "The Real Video-Game Wars," *Wall Street Journal,* March 20, 2000

Stratagem 3: Invite your enemy onto the roof, then remove the ladder

Tichy, Noel M., *Control Your Destiny or Someone Else Will* (New York: Harper Business, 2001)

Bibliography

"Encyclopedia Britannica Makes Some Changes," *Information Today*, July 2001

"Microsoft Encarta: Multimedia Encyclopedia on CD-Rom," review in *Online Libraries & Microcomputers Intelligence*, June 1993

Beckham, David "The Evolution of Encarta," *CD-ROM World*, 1993

"Education and Reference Best-Sellers," *Computer Life*, December 1994

Stratagem 4: Lure the tiger down from the mountain

D'Aveni, Richard, *Hypercompetition* (New York: Free Press, 1994)

Stratagem 5: Befriend the distant enemy to attack one nearby

Takahashi, Dean, "The Game of War," *Red Herring*, October 15, 2001

Norton, Leslie P. "Toy Soldiers: Can Microsoft Beat Sony and Nintendo at their own Game?," *Barron's*, May 14, 2001 www.hoovers.com

Stratagem 6: Kill with a borrowed knife

Brandenburger, Adam, and Barry Nalebuff, "The Right Game," *Harvard Business Review*, July-August 1995

Stratagem 7: Besiege Wei to rescue Zhao

"Despite the Jitters, Most Coffeehouses Survive Starbucks," *Wall Street Journal*, September 24, 2002, 1

Stratagem 8: The stratagem of sowing discord

Cabral, Luis "The Venezuelan Cola Wars," *Financial Times*, August 20, 1996

Fischer, Jeff "Fool Portfolio Report," *Motley Fool*, December 4, 1996

Stratagem 9: Trouble the water to catch the fish

Brandenburger, Adam M. and Nalebuff, Barry J. *Coopetition: A Revolutionary Mindset that Combines Competition and Co-Operation: The Game Theory Strategy that's Changing the Game of Business* (New York: Doubleday, 1996)

II. Wu Wei/Go with the grain

Stratagem 10: Remove the firewood from under the pot

Porter, Michael, *Competitive Advantage* (New York: Free Press, 1985)

Brandenburger, Adam M. and Nalebuff, Barry J. *Coopetition: A Revolutionary Mindset that Combines Competition and Co-Operation: The Game Theory Strategy that's Changing the Game of Business* (New York: Doubleday, 1996)

Stratagem 11: Shut the door to capture the thief

Norton, Leslie P. "Toy Soldiers: Can Microsoft Beat Sony and Nintendo at Their Own Game?" *Barrons*, May 14, 2001

Brandenburger, Adam M. and Nalebuff, Barry J. *Coopetition: A Revolutionary Mindset that Combines Competition and Co-Operation: The Game Theory Strategy that's*

Changing the Game of Business (New York: Doubleday, 1996)

Stratagem 12: Replace the beams with rotten timbers

Norton, Leslie, P. "Can Microsoft Beat Sony and Nintendo at their Own Game?," *Barron's*, May 14, 2001, p. 25

Stratagem 13: The stratagem of the beautiful woman

"Microsoft: How it Became Stronger than Ever," *Business Week*, June 4, 2001.

Stratagem 14: Beat the grass to startle the snake

Peter Lewis, "AOL vs. Microsoft," *Fortune Magazine*, July 23, 2001.

Jay Greene, Steve Hamm, Catherine Yang, and Irene M. Kunii, "On to the Living Room! Can Microsoft Control the digital home?" *Business Week Magazine,* January 21, 2002

Stratagem 15: Loot a burning house

Goerne, "Häagen-Dazs Adds Flavors to Ice Its Superpremium Competitors," *Marketing News*, August 31, 1992.

Maremont, "They're All Screaming for Häagen-Dazs," *Business Week*, October 14, 1991.

Hwang, Suein, L. "While Many Competitors See Sales Melt, Ben & Jerry's Scoops Out Solid Growth," *Wall Street Journal*, May 25, 1993.

Foust, Dean; Smith, Geri; Rocks, David, "Coke's Man on the Spot," *Business Week,* May 3, 1999.

Stratagem 16: Sometimes running away is the best strategy

Tichy, Noel M., *Control Your Destiny or Someone Else Will*, (New York: Harper Business, 2001)

Stratagem 17: Seize the opportunity to lead the sheep away

Drucker, Peter, *Innovation and Entrepreneurship*, (New York: Harper & Row, 1986)

Kim and Mauborgne, "Creating New Market Space," *Harvard Business Review* Jan-Feb 1999, pp. 84–85.

Stratagem 18: Feign madness but keep your balance

Branson, Richard, *Losing My Virginity* (London: Virgin Publishing 1998)

III. WU CHANG/ CONTINUOUS CHANGE

Stratagem 19: Watch the fire on the other shore

Webster's New Universal Unabridged Dictionary, Random House Value Publishing, 1996.

Brandenburger, Adam M. and Nalebuff, Barry J. *Coopetition: A Revolutionary Mindset that Combines Competition and Co-Operation: The Game Theory Strategy that's Changing the Game of Business* (New York: Doubleday, 1996)

Bruce Gilley, "Strategies—Branson's Big Bet: With Huge investments and high hopes, Richard Branson turns to Asia to reinvigorate his Virgin Group," *Far Eastern Economic Review* October 12, 2000.

Stratagem 20: Let the plum tree wither in place of the peach

Conference notes from The Cohre Conference, University of California, Berkley, May 17, 1999, presentation: *Competing on the Edge* by Kathleen Eisenhardt, Professor of Strategy and Organization, Stanford University.

Meredith Livinson, "GE: Destruction Pays Off" *CIO Magazine*, October 15, 2001

Stratagem 21: The stratagem of the open city gates

"Companies That Compete Best," *Fortune Magazine*, May 22, 1989.

David B. Yoffie and Mary Kwak, *Judo Strategy*, Harvard Business School Press, 2001.

Stratagem 22: Await the exhausted enemy at your ease

Kokuryo, Jiro "Asahi Breweries, Ltd." Harvard Business School case 9–389–114, published 1989, revised October 12, 1994.

Author-conducted interview with CEO of a South Asian apparel manufacturer July 25, 2001

Stratagem 24: Borrow the road to conquer Gao

Marshal, Tyler "Little-Known PC Maker Is Legend in the Making," *Los Angeles Times*, September 2, 2001.

Author-conducted interview with former Sinotrans executive, March 1999.

D'Aveni, Richard, *Hypercompetition* (New York: Free Press, 1994)

Stratagem 25: Shed your skin like the golden secada

Holmes, Stanley "A Test of Faith for Boeing's Believers," *Business Week*, September 25, 2001

Streets, J., "Thomson Travel Group Company Report," Warburg Dillon Read analyst report, July 1, 1998.

Stratagem 26: The stratagem of injuring yourself

Brandenburger, Adam M. and Nalebuff, Barry J. *Coopetition: A Revolutionary Mindset that Combines Competition and Co-Operation: The Game Theory Strategy that's Changing the Game of Business* (New York: Doubleday, 1996)

Stratagem 27: Borrow a corpse for the soul's return

W. Chan Kim and Renee Mauborgne, "How Southwest Airlines Found a Route to Success," *The Financial Times*, May 13, 1999

Slywotzky, Adrian, and David Morrison, *The Profit Zone*, (New York: Times Books, 1998), 70

IV. SHANG BING WU BING/INDIRECT ACTION

Stratagem 28: Point at the mulberry but curse the locust

Internet Movie Database (www.imdb.com).

Goldsmith, Charles "British Airways's No-Frills Carrier, Go, to Battle Its New Discount Rivals," *Wall Street Journal,* May 22, 1998.

Stratagem 29: Clamor in the east; attack to the west

Franks, Julian and Mayer, Colin, *Bank Control, Takeovers and Corporate Governance in Germany,* (Oxford: Comparative Corporate Governance, Clarendon Press, 1998)

Stratagem 30: Openly repair the walkway, secretly march to Chen Cang

Hindustan-Lever 2001 annual report

"Strategic Innovation: Hindustan Lever Ltd.," *Fast Company,* issue 47, page 120, source: www.fastcompany.com

Stratagem 31: Fool the emperor and cross the sea

Franks, Julian, and Colin Mayer, *Bank Control, Takeovers and Corporate Governance in Germany,* (Oxford: Comparative Corporate Governance, Clarendon Press, 1998)

McKechnie, Gary, "The Birth of Walt Disney World," *Fodors.com,* January 24, 2001

Dixit, Avinash K. and Nalebuff, Barry J., *Thinking Strategically,* (New York and London: W. W. Norton, 1991), 353

Stratagem 32: Create something out of nothing

D'Aveni, Richard, *Strategic Supremacy* (New York: Free Press, 2001)

Moriguchi and Lane, "A Hundred-Year War: Coke vs. Pepsi, 1890s–1990s," Harvard Business School Case No. 9–799–117, January 14, 2000

"Pepsi to Spin Off Bottling Group," *Atlanta Journal and Constitution,* January 9, 1999

International Directory of Company Histories (St. James Press, 1990), 128–130

Brandenburger, Adam M. and Nalebuff, Barry J. *Coopetition: A Revolutionary Mindset that Combines Competition and Co-Operation: The Game Theory Strategy that's Changing the Game of Business* (New York: Doubleday, 1996)

Mao Tse-tung, *On Guerilla Warfare,* translated by Griffith II, Samuel B., *On Guerilla Warfare* (Urbana and Chicago, IL: University of Illinois Press, 1961)

Stratagem 33: Hide a dagger behind a smile

Robert, Michel, *Strategy Pure and Simple II* (New York: McGraw Hill, 1997), 145

D'Aveni, Richard, *Hypercompetition* (New York: Free Press, 1994)

Stratagem 34: Deck the tree with bogus blossoms

D'Aveni, Richard, *Hypercompetition* (New York: Free Press, 1994)

Sratagem 35: To catch the bandits, capture their leader

"Dutch Court Orders Probe Of Gucci 'Mismanagement'—LVMH Praises Ruling as It

Continues Effort to Derail $3 Billion PPR Deal," *Wall Street Journal*, March 9, 2001

Kamm, Thomas "LVMH Will Turn to Court To Seek Control of Gucci," *Asian Wall Street Journal*, April 9, 1999

Kamm, Thomas and Barrett, Amy "Gucci Ordered to Study LVMH's Bid Plan," *Asian Wall Street Journal*, March 23, 1999

Ball, Deborah "PPR Files Complaint in Paris Against LVMH—Luxury-Goods Giant Is Accused of Defamation," *Asian Wall Street Journal*, December 1, 2000

KAIHAN KRIPPENDORFF SPENT THREE years as a consultant and manager at McKinsey & Company, helping leading corporations craft winning strategies. Prior to McKinsey, Kaihan held various senior positions in investment banking, consulting, and management. He earned his MBA from Columbia Business School and London Business School, his BSE in Finance from the University of Pennsylvania's Wharton School, and his BSE in Engineering from the University of Pennsylvania's School of Engineering. He lives in Miami, Florida where he writes, consults, teaches, and leads a non-profit organization.

ABOUT THE TYPE

The text of this book was set in Adobe Minion, a typeface designed by Robert Slimbach and issued as a digital original by the Adobe Corporation in 1989. It is a typeface of neohumanist design, inspired by the classical, old-style types of the late Renaissance.

Printed and bound by Edwards Brothers, Inc.,
Ann Arbor, Michigan

Designed and composed by Kevin Hanek